Readings on
THE SIX YOGAS OF NAROPA

Readings on
THE SIX YOGAS OF NAROPA

Translated, edited and introduced
by Glenn H. Mullin

Snow Lion Publications
Ithaca, New York, USA

Snow Lion Publications
P.O. Box 6483
Ithaca, New York 14851 USA
607-273-8519

Printed in Canada.

ISBN 1-55939-074-3

Library of Congress Cataloging-in-Publication Data

Readings on the six yogas of Naropa / translated, edited and introduced by Glenn
    H. Mullin
        p.   cm.
    Includes bibliographical references.
    ISBN 1-55939-074-3
    1. Na⁻ap›da. 2. Yoga (Tantric Buddhism)   I. Mullin, Glenn H.
    BQ7950.N347R43   1997
    294.3'4436--dc21   97-18938
                                                                      CIP

Table of Contents

Preface

Although it is complete in its own right and stands well on its own, this collection of short commentaries on the Six Yogas of Naropa, translated from the Tibetan, was originally conceived of as a companion reader to my *Tsongkhapa's Six Yogas of Naropa* (Snow Lion, 1996).

That volume presents one of the greatest Tibetan treatises on the Six Yogas system, a text composed by the Tibetan master Lama Jey Tsongkhapa (1357-1419)—*A Book of Three Inspirations: A Treatise on the Stages of Training in the Profound Path of Naropa's Six Yogas* (Tib. *Zab lam na ro'i chos drug gi 'khrid yig yid ches gsum ldan*) (hereafter referred to as *A Book of Three Inspirations*). Lama Jey Tsongkhapa was the founder of the eclectic Geluk school and the root guru of the First Dalai Lama (1391-1475). The introduction to that work gives a lengthy summary of the history and contents of the tradition of the Six Yogas of Naropa, which is not repeated here.

The work of preparing *Tsongkhapa's Six Yogas of Naropa* led me to read over a dozen classical Indian and Tibetan treatments of the Six Yogas. Six of those texts are included here: a brief verse work by the Indian mahasiddha Tilopa (988-1069), who is regarded as the original formulator of the system of the Six Yogas; a slightly longer verse work by Tilopa's chief disciple, known to history as Pandita Naropa (1016-1100), after whom the system is named; a commentary found in Lama Jey Tsongkhapa's *Collected Works* (Tib. *gSung 'bum*), entitled *A Practice Manual on the Six Yogas of Naropa: Taking the Practice in Hand* (Tib. *Na ro'i chos drug gi dmigs skor lag tu len tshul*, hereafter referred to as *A Practice Manual on the Six Yogas*), which is much shorter in length than his formal treatise and focuses exclusively on the yogic techniques and meditations of the tradition; Gyalwa Wensapa's (1505-1566) presentation of "the three blendings," an important aspect of and also an alternative name for the Six Yogas; the First Panchen Lama's (1568-1662) treatment of the yogas, which emphasizes the first and fourth of the six yogas, i.e., the yogas of inner heat and of consciousness transference; and, lastly, a small text found in the collected works of the nineteenth-century lama Jey Sherab Gyatso (1803-1875), which was compiled by one of his disciples from a public discourse given by Jey Sherab Gyatso in 1836 on Tsongkhapa's *A Book of Three Inspirations*.

The above list of the six texts is in the order of their historical appearance as literary compositions. In this volume, however, I have placed the works by Jey Sherab Gyatso and Gyalwa Wensapa respectively as Chapters Three and Four, thus arranging them before the works by Tsongkhapa and the First Panchen Lama, who lived earlier in history than they. My logic in arranging them in this way is that the texts by Tilopa and Naropa in Chapters One and Two, although brief, show the roots of the tradition. Jey Sherab Gyatso's *Notes* in Chapter Three works well as an introduction to the overall approach taken to the Six Yogas, and describes how the general Buddhist trainings are used to prepare the mind of the practitioner for tantric endeavor. Gyalwa Wensapa's treatise in Chapter Four presents the underlying dynamic on which the Six Yogas tradition is based, namely "the three blendings." Lama Tsongkhapa's *A Practice Manual on the Six Yogas* in Chapter Five presents the nuts and bolts of the actual yogic disciplines. Finally, the First Panchen Lama's text in Chapter Six provides an excellent summary of the tradition, with emphasis on the inner heat and consciousness transference yogas.

These six translations were prepared with the guidance and assistance of various lama friends. When studying Tsongkhapa's *A Book of Three Inspirations* with Ven. Doboom Tulku, one of my root gurus, we also looked at parts of Tsongkhapa's *A Practice Manual on the Six Yogas*. A few months later I carefully read through this latter text with Ven. Ngawang Pendey, a wonderful Dharma friend from Drepung Loseling. With Ngawang Pendey I also read through several short commentaries on Tsongkhapa's *A Book of Three Inspirations*, including that by Jey Sherab Gyatso which forms the substance of Chapter Three, and also Gyalwa Wensapa's *Handprints of the Path of the Six Yogas of Naropa: A Source of Every Realization*, herein placed as Chapter Four. Later I rechecked several sections of these works with Geshey Lobzang Tenzin, also of Drepung Loseling. The texts by Tilopa and Naropa, and also the treatise by the First Panchen Lama, were prepared a year later while I was on a teaching tour in Italy. There the most learned and accomplished master Geshey Jampa Gyatso of Sera Jey Monastery, a lord of the Six Yogas tradition who for the past almost twenty years has been the resident teacher at Istituto Lama Tzong Khapa near Pisa, kindly made time in his busy schedule to nurse my understanding through these intensely terse and difficult works, and also took time to re-read difficult passages of the other texts in this volume. His wisdom, learning, humor and profound realization brought out their essence like butter churned from milk.

A number of Western friends also helped me in getting the manuscript into its final form. Jimmy Apple at the University of Wisconsin checked dates and historical references. Pierre Robillard and Michael Wurmbrand did some indispensable leg work on obscure points in the texts. Lulu Hamlin, Hilary Shearman, Debby Spencer and Renee Turolla offered useful suggestions. Finally, as always, my seven children fired my imagination and provided much inspiration.

It is my hope that these six translations will give tantric enthusiasts a sense of the esoteric and profound nature of the tradition known in Tibetan as the *Naro Choe Druk*, as well as of its historical continuity.

Technical Note

The authors whose works are translated in this volume frequently quote Indian and Tibetan texts. Throughout the volume these titles are simplified for the benefit of the general reader but are listed in a more formal manner at the back of the volume. The first section of the list of texts quoted gives Indian texts and includes both the original sutras and tantras taught by the Buddha and the treatises by later Indian masters. The second section contains indigenous Tibetan works.

The original tantras taught by the Buddha are usually named after a particular mandala deity, and generally in the text I have put these in an abbreviated Anglicized Sanskrit. An example is *The Hevajra Tantra*. The titles of texts by later Indian masters generally are more translatable into English, and therefore I have taken the liberty of doing so with them. An example is *The Five Stages* by the Indian master Nagarjuna. The titles of indigenous Tibetan works also seem to translate well into English; an example is Tsongkhapa's *A Lamp on the Five Stages*.

Throughout the text Tibetan personal and place names appear as they are pronounced and not as they are formally spelled, due to the number of silent letters used in Tibetan syllables, for example, "Khedrub Norzang Gyatso" rather than "mKhas sgrub nor bzang rgya mtsho." Those wishing to check the formal spellings can refer to the glossary at the back of the volume.

I have not provided a glossary of technical terms. The few words that I feel the reader will benefit from knowing in Sanskrit or Tibetan are given in parentheses where they appear in the text. Tantric Buddhism speaks in a straightforward language, and very little of it is beyond the range of the English language. The aim of tantric literature is to inspire and guide spiritual seekers in the universal doctrine of enlightenment. The more Western readers can integrate it into their own linguistic environment, the greater will be their ability to demystify it and thus to integrate its inner essence into their own lives.

Translator's Introduction

THE *NARO CHOE DRUK*

The tradition known in Tibet as the *Naro Choe Druk* (Tib. *Na ro'i chos drug*) translates literally as "Naro's Six Doctrines," but has become better known to Western students of Tibetan Buddhism as "the Six Yogas of Naropa." Early scholars such as Dr. Evans-Wentz, Prof. Herbert Guenther, and Garma C.C. Chang used this rendition in their translations and consequently established it as standard in the Western Buddhist world. Therefore I have followed their lead in using the term "Six Yogas," rather than "Six Doctrines," both in my earlier work and in the present compendium.

Over the centuries the manner in which the Six Yogas have been taught has varied with the different lines of transmission. Lama Jey Tsongkhapa discusses this in some depth in his longer commentary. There are also traditions of speaking of two, three, four, six, eight, and ten yogas of Naropa. However, these variations are merely different ways of dividing up the pie of the Naropa yogas; there are no substantial differences in what is taught.

To accommodate these differing modes of structuring the Naropa system, in both his longer and shorter treatises Lama Jey Tsongkhapa uses a somewhat complex system of outlines and headings. He does not simply present the six yogas in six chapters, but instead weaves a subtle line of thought that flows through his entire presentation. This makes his two treatises somewhat more difficult to follow than many of the simpler manuals on the system, but accommodates very accurately the flexible nature of the tradition and reflects the arbitrariness of calling it the "Six Yogas."

Later Gelukpa commentaries generally follow Tsongkhapa's lead in this respect. They rarely treat the Six Yogas in six chapters.

THE BACKGROUND AND NATURE OF THE PRACTICE

The Geluk school, which was formed in the early fifteenth century as a fusion of lineages from a dozen earlier sects, received its transmission of the Six Yogas primarily from the Zhalu (Sakya) school. The Zhalu had received it from the Drikung Kargyu (one of the Eight Younger Kargyu schools), which in turn is a derivative of the Pakmo Drupa Kargyu (one of the Four Older Kargyu schools). The Geluk lineage presents the Six Yogas in accordance with the way they were transmitted by Lama Pal Pakmo Drupa, the founder of the Pakmo Drupa school, to Lama Drikung Jigten Sumgon, the founder of the Drikung Kargyu school.

According to Lama Pal Pakmo Drupa's lineage the six yogas are listed as follows: inner heat yoga; illusory body yoga; clear light yoga; the yoga for the transference of consciousness to a higher realm; the yoga for transference of consciousness into another body; and the bardo yoga.

In this arrangement of the six, the inner heat is the foundation of all the yogas; the illusory body and clear light yogas are grouped together as the actual or principal practices for inducing the experience of enlightenment; and the yogas of consciousness transference to a higher realm and transference into another body are auxiliary or branch applications. This accounts for five of the six; the sixth, or bardo yoga, is regarded as both a branch of the illusory body yoga and as a third auxiliary practice.

In other words, the first three yogas—inner heat, illusory body and clear light—are the real methods for accomplishing enlightenment in one lifetime. The last three yogas—consciousness transference to a higher realm, transference into another body, and the bardo yoga—are only required if one fails to accomplish enlightenment before death draws near, and a forceful last-minute method of self-protection is required. The First Panchen Lama puts it as follows in his *The Golden Key: A Profound Guide to the Six Yogas of Naropa*:

> The idea is that if one is not able to accomplish all the practices leading to enlightenment before death comes to destroy one's body-vessel, then in order to fulfill the purposes of oneself and others one engages the yogas of either consciousness transference

or projection into another body. Alternatively, if one is unable to effect this transference, or if one wishes instead to attempt to accomplish final enlightenment in the bardo, then there is the doctrine of the bardo yogas.

In both his longer and shorter treatises on the Six Yogas system (*A Book of Three Inspirations* and *A Practice Manual on the Six Yogas*) Lama Jey Tsongkhapa dedicates special attention to the first of the six, or inner heat yoga, because success in the remaining five depends on the level of proficiency attained in the inner heat practice. As he explains in *A Book of Three Inspirations*,

In general, all systems of highest yoga tantra's completion stage involve the preliminary process of controlling the vital energies flowing through the two side channels, *rasana* and *lalana*, and redirecting them into the central channel, *avadhuti*. This is indispensable.

There are numerous means for accomplishing this, based on the traditions of the Indian mahasiddhas, who drew from the various tantric systems. In this tradition [i.e., the Six Yogas of Naropa] the main technique is to arouse the inner heat at the navel chakra, the "wheel of emanation," and then through controlling the life energies by means of the *AH*-stroke mantric syllable, to draw the subtle life-sustaining energies into the central channel. When these energies enter the central channel the four blisses are induced, and one cultivates meditation on the basis of these in such a way as to give rise to the innate wisdom of mahamudra....

In this tradition the expression "the inner heat, the foundation stone," is well known. This is because in the completion stage yogas one uses the inner heat technology from the very beginning in order to collect the subtle life-sustaining energies into the central channel and thereby arouse the innate great bliss. This is the actual basis upon which all practices rely and upon which all later completion stage yogas are founded. The inner heat doctrine establishes this basis.

The practice of the inner heat doctrine entails directing the life-sustaining energies into the central channel. Here the energies enter, abide, and are dissolved. When one trains well in this technique, the strength of the experience has the power to give control over loss of the bodhimind substance [i.e., the sexual drops]. Then, based on this power, one can rely upon a karmamudra as a conducive condition to arouse the four blisses. On this foundation, innate bliss is aroused. Arousing this innate bliss is the purpose of the practices of the inner heat yoga and karmamudra.

One unites the innate bliss with [meditation upon] emptiness, and during the waking state applies oneself to the illusory body doctrine. Based on the experience of the illusory body practice one can engage in the clear light techniques.

Then when asleep at night one can cultivate awareness of the illusory nature of dreams. To do so effectively one must first master the yoga of retaining the clear light of sleep [i.e., the clear light that arises at the moment of falling asleep], and then enter into the dream state from that perspective. If the power to retain the clear light of sleep is accomplished by means of gaining control over the vital energies, this means that during the time of waking practice one must have mastered this control and cultivated the ability to direct the energies into the central channel. Thus the foundation stone of both practices [sleep and dream yogas] is the inner heat doctrine.

Only when progress in dream yoga has been made firm can one effectively work with the bardo yogas. Thus here again [with the bardo yogas] the foundation stone is the power achieved through the inner heat....

As for the yogas of special consciousness transference and forceful projection, as a preliminary to them one must cultivate the ability to draw the life-sustaining energies into the central channel. Therefore in these two the inner heat yoga again is the foundation stone.

Thus the inner heat yoga is the basis for success in the remaining five yogas. For this reason Tsongkhapa and most later Gelukpa commentators made the elucidation of this yoga their prime concern.

In recent centuries most treatises written by the Tibetan lamas of the twelve Kargyu schools drop out the fifth yoga—that of forceful projection into another body—because the Naropa lineage of this yoga allegedly was lost with the death of Marpa's son Darma Dodey. They make up the list of six by separating dream yoga from the illusory body yogas and treat it by itself.

Tsongkhapa, however, like Pal Pakmo Drupa, taught dream yoga as one of the three stages of the illusory body training, and this tradition has continued in Gelukpa commentarial literature. He provides a detailed account of the forceful projection yoga in *A Book of Three Inspirations*, but in *A Practice Manual on the Six Yogas* he simply mentions the yoga by name and does not elucidate the practice, presumably because he considers it beyond the abilities and concerns of most people.

This having been said, it is important to remember that, even though the Naropa lineage of the forceful projection yoga may perhaps have died out (and even this theory is questionable), the source of the technique is *The Chaturpita Tantra*, which, together with its oral transmission, still survives.

Whatever the case may be, the forceful projection yoga is undoubtedly the least used of any of the Six Yogas, and is really only maintained out of honor to the masters of the past.

EARLY LITERATURE ON THE SIX YOGAS

Although it is generally stated that the Indian mahasiddha Tilopa formulated the tradition of the Six Yogas and transmitted it to Naropa, and also that Naropa transmitted the tradition to his Tibetan disciple Marpa Lotsawa, who imported it into Tibet, there is not much literature on the Six Yogas from this early period. The Nartang *Tengyur*, or canonical collection of texts by Indian Buddhist masters that were translated from Sanskrit into Tibetan, contains only one short verse work by Tilopa on the subject (included here as Chapter One), and nothing by Naropa. The Dergey Tengyur, which is an alternative canonical collection published in Eastern Tibet several generations later, contains the same text by Tilopa, and also one slightly longer work by Naropa (included here as Chapter Two).

It would also seem that Marpa Lotsawa, who brought the lineage to Tibet in the mid-eleventh century, did not write much on the Six Yogas. Tsongkhapa mentions in *A Book of Three Inspirations* that some Tibetans do attribute one work to him; but the manner in which he refers to the matter suggests that it is a controversial subject and that most lamas do not accept the authenticity of the claim. Nor did Marpa's immediate disciple Milarepa write on the system. As Tsongkhapa puts it in *A Book of Three Inspirations*,

> Two fundamental texts serve as the basis of the Six Yogas of Naropa: *The Early Compendium Root Text* and *The Later Compendium Root Text*.[1] It seems that there are two major problems with the former work. Some commentaries say that the second one was compiled by Lama Marpa himself.... We see such statements made, but it is difficult to ascertain their veracity.
>
> Another work attributed to Lama Marpa is entitled *The Eight Instructions,* which blends verse and prose in its presentation. Then there is *The Vajra Song of the Six Yogas.* However, these two are only intended to plant the seeds of the oral tradition teachings and are too brief to do much more than that.

The reason for this terseness in the early literature on the Six Yogas is that in those days the system was taught purely as an ear-whispered transmission teaching (Tib. *snyan brgyud*). As Lama Tsongkhapa states, these brief written works were mainly intended to place seeds on the mindstream of the disciple, not to serve as practical guides. This latter function would have been performed by an oral teaching received directly from a lineage holder.

In later centuries, however, the Six Yogas became the subject of much literary activity, and hundreds of commentaries appeared. This was not a matter of the Tibetans becoming sloppy in their attitudes toward tantric secrecy, but rather was a fulfillment of an instruction given by Naropa himself.

In a concluding verse to his text *Vajra Verses of the Whispered Tradition*, Naropa wrote,

> For thirteen generations[2] this teaching
> Should be sealed in secrecy as an oral transmission.
> It is the essence of all sutras and tantras
> And brings liberation to the fortunate; therefore
> It should be used to accomplish the meaningful.

Thus Naropa clearly states that for thirteen generations in Tibet the transmission of the Six Yogas should be treated with great secrecy, and passed exclusively as an oral tradition, i.e., should not be written out in detail. The implication is that after that time the world would be ready for it to become the subject of commentarial literature.

It is significant that Lama Jey Tsongkhapa, perhaps the greatest writer in Tibetan history, belonged to the fourteenth generation of Tibetan masters, which was the first generation to be allowed to write openly on the Six Yogas. His two texts greatly contributed to the preservation of the tradition, as well as to the popularity that the Six Yogas achieved over the succeeding centuries.

Here Tilopa and Naropa are not included in the count of thirteen generations, because the instruction of "secrecy for thirteen generations" was given by Naropa to his disciple Marpa, making Marpa the first of the thirteen.

The names of the early Tibetan masters in the line of transmission that passed from generation to generation and eventually came to Lama Jey Tsongkhapa are as follows: (1) Marpa Lotsawa, who received the transmission from Naropa; (2) Milarepa, the most important of the three disciples to receive the lineage from Marpa; (3) Gampopa, the most successful of Milarepa's two chief disciples; (4) Pal Pakmo Drupa, founder of the Pakmo Drupa Kargyu school and the chief of Gampopa's four main disciples (each of whom formed one of the "Four Older Kargyu schools"); (5) Drikung Jigten Sumgon, founder of the Drikung Kargyu school and the senior of Pal Pakmo Drupa's eight chief disciples (each of whom formed one of the "Eight Younger Kargyu schools"); (6) Tsangpa Rechung, an early Drikung Kargyu master; (7) Jampa Palwa, also of the Drikung Kargyu; (8) Sonam Wangpo, another yogi of the Drikung Kargyu to achieve enlightenment in one lifetime; (9) Sonam Sengey, a lion amongst yogis; (10) Yangtsewa, one of the Drikung Kargyu's most talented and prolific writers; (11) Bu-ton Rinchen Drubpa, a lama of the Sakya school, from whom is traced the Zhalu school; (12) Khedrub Jampa Pel, Bu-ton's main Dharma heir in the Six Yogas transmission; (13) Lama Drakpa Jangchup, a Zhalu lama of great renown; and (14) Lama Jey Tsongkhapa, founder of Ganden Monastery and the Geluk school.[3]

Thus Lama Jey Tsongkhapa belongs to the fourteenth generation in the Tibetan line of transmission, and as such was free to write extensively on the system.

ORIGINAL SOURCES OF THE SIX YOGAS

As with all Buddhist teachings, tradition claims that the original source of the Six Yogas of Naropa is none other than the Buddha himself, who 2,500 years ago taught many different sutras and tantras, the former being his open discourses and the latter his secret Vajrayana discourses. The Six Yogas of Naropa is a synthesis of numerous tantric doctrines embodied in the original tantras taught by the Buddha. This is explained by Lama Tsongkhapa in *A Book of Three Inspirations*,

> The instruction on the inner heat yoga comes to us through Tilopa, who commented that this was the transmission of the mahasiddha Krishnacharya, also known [to Tibetans] as Lobpon Acharyapa, which fuses [the teachings on inner heat yoga found in] the *Hevajra Tantra* and the *Heruka Chakrasamvara Tantra*....
>
> The illusory body and the clear light doctrines are derived from the oral tradition teachings of the *Guhyasamaja Tantra*, as transmitted through the Indian mahasiddha Jnanagarbha. This Marpa tradition of the Guhyasamaja oral instruction transmission has been used as the basis, with embellishments from the Guhyasamaja transmission of the Aryas, Father and Sons [i.e., Nagarjuna and his disciples Aryadeva and Chandrakirti].
>
> The practices of consciousness transference and forceful projection to a new residence are based primarily on the *Shri Chaturpita Tantra*.[4]

Thus all six of the Naropa yogas are sourced in original tantric texts taught by the Buddha. The inner heat yoga is a fusion of those practices taught in the *Hevajra Tantra* and the *Heruka Chakrasamvara Tantra*;

the illusory body and clear light yogas are based on the *Guhyasamaja Tantra*; and both consciousness transference and forceful projection yogas are based on the *Shri Chaturpita Tantra*. All of these original tantras were taught by the Buddha. Here Lama Tsongkhapa does not mention the bardo yoga separately, for in the Six Yogas tradition this is treated as an extension of the illusory body yoga, and thus is also based on the *Guhyasamaja Tantra*.

All of these original tantras were translated from Sanskrit into Tibetan and are preserved in the Kangyur canon. In addition, numerous commentaries to them by later Indian masters are preserved in the Tengyur. Tsongkhapa points out that for the Six Yogas tradition the most important of the Indian commentaries is Krishnacharya's treatise on the inner heat yoga.

THE NAME OF THE TRANSMISSION

As we will see later in Chapter One, which contains Tilopa's brief verse work on the Six Yogas, Tilopa primarily drew from four Indian lineages in formulating the system that would become known to history as the Six Yogas. The title of his text was probably given retroactively by the Tibetans; it is a guide to what is known as "Tilopa's Four Instructions," which when translated into yogic practice become the Six Yogas.

The title of the slightly longer verse work by Tilopa's Indian disciple Naropa, after whom the Tibetans named the system, was probably also given retroactively by the Tibetans. This is indicated by the fact that in the early days of the lineage in Tibet there were traditions of speaking of two, three, four, six, eight and ten yogas. Had both Tilopa and Naropa spoken specifically of six yogas, as the names of their two texts would seem to imply, the Tibetans would automatically have followed this lead, and there would not be a tradition of speaking of differing numbers of yogas. In fact the name of the text given in its colophon is *The Vajra Verses: An Instruction to Jnana Dakini*; the official title under which it appears in the Tengyur—*Vajra Verses of the Whispered Tradition*—is not mentioned in the text itself.

In all probability it was Milarepa's chief disciple Gampopa, whose work produced the Dakpo Kargyu school (which later branched into the Four Older and Eight Younger Kargyu subsects), who popularized the name the "Six Yogas of Naropa." A brief treatise using the name "the Six Yogas" appears in his Collected Works. Of course the phrase also exists in Milarepa's biography; but this was composed several generations later and again probably introduces the terminology retroactively.

It seems that Marpa and Milarepa mostly referred to the lineage as "the Oral Instruction Transmission for Achieving Liberation in the Bardo." Lama Jey Tsongkhapa refers to this name in the introductory section of his longer commentary, *A Book of Three Inspirations*, wherein he discusses the necessity for achieving maturity in the basic Buddhist practices before engaging in advanced tantric trainings such as the Six Yogas of Naropa. He writes,

> It is recorded that when Venerable Milarepa taught the oral instruction transmission for achieving liberation in the bardo he said, "First establish the basics, such as Refuge in the Three Jewels, the two aspects of the enlightenment mind—aspirational and engaged—and so forth.[5] Otherwise both [guru and disciple] will fall over the precipice of spiritual disaster, like two oxen yoked together...."
>
> The above expression "the oral instruction transmission for achieving liberation in the bardo" is synonymous [with the Six Yogas of Naropa].[6]

In Chapter Four we will see more on this name for the Six Yogas tradition, "the oral instruction transmission for achieving liberation in the bardo," when Gyalwa Wensapa, a wonderful fifteenth-century Gelukpa lama and yogi who spent much of his life in retreat, discusses the Six Yogas from the perspective of how they relate to the process of blending the three kayas with the three bardos, or in-between states: the bardo of waking state consciousness; the bardo of sleep and dreams; and the bardo between death and rebirth. This process is also known as "the three blendings," which is another name for the Six Yogas system.

THE LIVING TRADITION

The Six Yogas of Naropa has inspired meditators of Central Asia for a thousand years now, and continues to be as popular as ever. It is practiced to some extent in all sects of Tibetan Buddhism, although is especially popular in the Kargyu and Geluk schools. During the twelve years that I lived with the Tibetan refugees in India I had the wonderful fortune to encounter many yogis who were well established in the practice. There were always a dozen or so Gelukpa monks and nuns dedicated to the training who lived in the caves and huts in the mountains above Dharamsala. Forty miles southeast along the Himalayas, in the

Tibetan settlement of Tashi Jong, the long-haired *tokden* yogis of the Drukpa Kargyu school underwent six-year retreats in the Six Yogas. Another fifty miles southeast at Manali, high in the mountains of the Kulu Valley, His Eminence Apo Rinpochey constantly trained groups of Ladakhi monks in the system. Other groups pursued the Six Yogas training in other parts of the Himalayas. To mention but a few, there were Karma Kargyupas in the hills above Rumtek, Sikkim; Shangpa Kargyupas in the mountains above Darjeeling; Drikung Kargyupas in the caves and hermitages of Ladakh; Drukpa Kargyupas in Bhutan; and Nyingmapas in Nepal. All of these monks, nuns, yogis and yoginis upheld and continued the ancient lineage of the Six Yogas descending from Tilopa, Naropa, Marpa and Milarepa.

Each of the different schools of Tibetan Buddhism has developed the Six Yogas tradition in its own individual way and brought a unique character and flavor to the legacy. The Geluk school has made its own contributions in this respect, and I hope that my two books on the Six Yogas somewhat reflect this.

In *Tsongkhapa's Six Yogas of Naropa* I tried to convey a sense of the genius of Lama Jey Tsongkhapa and the vastness of his approach to the Six Yogas. In this collection of readings on the Six Yogas I am attempting to show how the original tradition as laid out by Tilopa and Naropa, and as clarified by Lama Jey Tsongkhapa, has continued to inspire practitioners over the centuries and has come into the present era with both depth and power.

1

The Oral Instruction of the Six Yogas

Skt. *Śatadharma-upadeśa-nāma*
Tib. *Chos drug gi man ngag zhes bya ba*

by

the Indian Mahasiddha Tilopa
988–1069 C.E.

Translator's Preamble

The Indian master Tilopa is regarded as the formulator of the Six Yogas system. He was born in 988 in Bengal to a brahmin family and as a youth helped support his family by tending buffaloes. This work gave him plenty of spare time, and as he sat in the fields with his herds he passed the hours first by learning to read and write, and then by studying and memorizing many of the great Buddhist scriptures. By the time he reached his teens he had become self-educated in the classics.

After he reached adulthood he journeyed to Oddiyana (the present-day Swat Valley of Pakistan), where he received numerous transmissions from a group of female mystics. Later he traveled widely and studied under many different Buddhist masters. He spent years in the intensive practice of meditation and eventually achieved enlightenment.[1]

His biography states that the main lineages he received and emphasized in his personal practice were the Madhyamaka doctrines and the *Guhyasamaja Tantra* transmissions descending from the mahasiddha Nagarjuna; the clear light and bardo doctrines of the mahasiddha Lawapa; the Heruka Chakrasamvara lineages descending from the mahasiddha Luipada; the Mahamudra lineages of the mahasiddha Shavari; and the inner heat doctrines of the *Hevajra Tantra* as transmitted through Krishnacharya.

In his later life Tilopa manifested countless miraculous activities in order to inspire and enlighten trainees. He could stop the sun in its path, shape-shift by changing himself into animal forms, fly through the sky, and visibly manifest tantric mandalas in space. Sometimes he lived quietly as a monk, and at others dwelled with corpses in charnel grounds. To provide conditions by which beings could collect merit he sometimes sustained himself by begging for alms, sometimes by operating a whore-house.

Tilopa's name, in the colophon to our text spelled "Tillipa," means "Sesame-seed Man." He earned this name because as a part of his enlightenment path he worked as a pounder of sesame seeds for producing oil, taking his work as a metaphor for how the oil of enlightenment is extracted from the seed of mundane experience. He had many disciples, but the greatest of all was Naropa, to whom he transmitted the Six Yogas that he had formulated.

Several short texts on the Six Yogas that are attributed to Tilopa exist in Tibetan, but only the verse work herein translated was considered authentic beyond question, and therefore was the only one to be included in the Tibetan canon of Indian commentaries, the Tengyur.

Tilopa's text is only a few verses in length but is nonetheless important in that it is the earliest known work on the Six Yogas. It mentions four important lineage masters from whom the Six Yogas had come to him: Krishnacharya, Nagarjuna, Lawapa and Sukhasiddhi. These four are the sources of the longer list given above, as gleaned from his biography.

In the translation I have added subheads giving the name of each of the six yogas. This may perhaps break the flow created by Tilopa's continuous style, but as compensation clarifies the ideas embodied in the work.

Tilopa's arrangement of the Six Yogas seems to be slightly different from that which became popular in Tibet in the Pakmo Drupa Kargyu school and subsequently in the Geluk. He lists them as (1) inner heat yoga from Krishnacharya, whom he refers to as Charyapa; (2) illusory body yoga from Nagarjuna; (3) dream yoga from Lawapa; (4) clear light yoga, also from Nagarjuna; (5) bardo yoga from Sukhasiddhi; and finally (6) the consciousness transference and forceful projection yogas, also from Sukhasiddhi.[2] My subheads indicate how they are grouped in the Pakmo Drupa Kargyu and Geluk schools.

The Oral Instruction of the Six Yogas

by the Indian Mahasiddha Tilopa

Homage to Glorious Chakrasamvara.[3]

Take advantage of the karmic process[4]
And extract the essence of the human potential.

INNER HEAT YOGA
The yogic body, a collection of energy channels,
Coarse and subtle, possessing the energy fields,
Is to be brought under control.
The method begins with the physical exercises.
The vital airs [i.e., energies] are drawn in,
Filled, retained and dissolved.
There are the two side channels,
The central channel *avadhuti*,
And the four chakras.
Flames rise from the *chandali* fire[5] at the navel.
A stream of nectar drips down
From the syllable *HAM* at the crown,
Invoking the four joys.
There are four results, like that similar to the cause,
And six exercises that expand them.
This is the instruction of Charyapa.[6]

ILLUSORY BODY YOGA
All animate and inanimate things of the three worlds
Are like the examples of an illusion, a dream and so forth.
See this at all times, both in movement and in stillness.
Contemplate an illusory deity reflected in a mirror;
Take a drawn image of Vajrasattva, and consider
How the reflected image vividly appears.
Just as that image is an illusory appearance,
So it is with all things.
The yogi thus contemplates the twelve similes
And sees the reality of how all things are illusory.
This is the instruction of Nagarjuna.[7]

Know dreams as dreams, and constantly
Meditate on their profound significance.
Visualize the seed syllables of the five natures
With the drop, the *nada* and so forth.
One perceives buddhas and buddhafields.
The time of sleep is the time for the method
That brings realization of great bliss.
This is the instruction of Lawapa.[8]

CLEAR LIGHT YOGA
The yogi working with the central channel
Places the mind in the central channel
And fixes concentration on the drop at the heart.
Visions arise, like lights, light-rays, rainbows,
The sunlight and moonlight at dawn,
The sun, the moon, and then
The appearances of deities and forms.
In this way the myriads of worlds are purified.
This most wondrous yogic path
Is the instruction of Nagarjuna.

BARDO YOGA
The yogi at the time of death withdraws
The energies of the senses and elements, and
Directs energies of sun and moon to the heart,
Giving rise to a myriad of yogic samadhis.

Consciousness goes to outer objects, but
He regards them as objects of a dream.
The appearances of death persist for seven days,
Or perhaps as much as seven times seven,
And then one must take rebirth.
At that time meditate on deity yoga
Or simply remain absorbed in emptiness.
After that, when the time comes for rebirth,
Use the deity yoga of a tantric master
And meditate on guru yoga with whatever appears.
Doing that will arrest the experience of the bardo.
This is the instruction of Sukhasiddhi.[9]

YOGAS OF CONSCIOUSNESS TRANSFERENCE
AND FORCEFUL PROJECTION

By means of these yogas, at the time of transference
And also of forceful projection into another body,
The yogi can utilize the mantric seed syllable of the deity
And train in the deity yoga practice in conjunction
With the exhalation and inhalation [of the breath], long and short,
And project consciousness to wherever is desired.
Alternatively, those desiring to transfer to a higher realm
Can apply themselves to two syllables of *YAM*, and also
HI-KA, and *HUM-HUM*.
Consciousness is thrown to the heart
Of the deity inseparable from the guru,
And from there to whatever buddhafield is desired.
This too is the instruction of Sukhasiddhi.

The colophon: Written from the words of the mahasiddha Tillipa; translated by the Indian sage Pandit Naropa and Marpa Lodrakpa Chokyi Lotru at the Kashmiri holy site known as Mount Pushpahara.

2

Vajra Verses of the Whispered Tradition

Skt. *Karṇatantra-vajrapāda-nāma*
Tib. *sNyan rgyud rdo rje'i tshig rkang*

by

the Indian Mahasiddha Naropa
1016–1100 C.E.

Translator's Preamble

Naropa is one of the most frequently quoted figures in Central Asian literature. Every Tibetan knows the major events of his life by heart, and lamas of all sects love to tell and re-tell the saga of his accomplishments as a monk, his renunciation of monastic life, his search for his tantric guru Tilopa, his dedication to and austere training under Tilopa, his achievement of enlightenment, and then his work in training disciples.

Born to an aristocratic family in 1016, in his youth he was forced into an arranged marriage. However, he soon left the worldly life and took the ordination of a Buddhist monk.

As a young renunciate he dedicated himself to intense study and practice. His learning and intellectual prowess became legendary, and by his early thirties he had risen in the Buddhist monastic hierarchy to the position of abbot of Nalanda, India's most prestigious monastic university. He retained the abbotship for some eight years, achieving widespread fame as one of India's foremost Buddhist scholars.

However, although his learning was unmatched, his inner realization was still incomplete. This became obvious to him when he was in his fortieth year. According to his biography, one day he was quietly reading a scripture when he noticed an ugly old woman observing him. She inquired, "Do you understand the words of what you are reading?" Naropa replied to the affirmative. The old hag laughed and added, "And do you understand the essence?" Again Naropa replied to the affirmative, whereupon the old woman burst out in tears. "Here you are lying," she scolded.

The traditional accounts state that the old hag was in fact a dakini, an angel in disguise, manifesting in order to guide him to the fulfillment of his destiny. The encounter profoundly affected Naropa, and he realized that his Buddhist understanding was merely intellectual. He resigned his seat in the monastery and left in search of a tantric guru.

This search led him through many adventures. Eventually, however, he met with Tilopa and entered into an intense twelve-year training under him. The feats of devotion and commitment that he had to manifest, and the many hardships that he underwent, have become the stuff of legend with Tibetans. Eventually, however, he achieved enlightenment.[1]

In his later life he in turn trained many disciples. The most famous of these in Tibetan literature is Marpa Lotsawa, a Tibetan translator who travelled to India three times and received the Six Yogas from him. It was Marpa Lotsawa who translated into Tibetan the brief text on the Six Yogas that follows, the authorship of which is attributed to Naropa.

Naropa's text on the Six Yogas was not included in the original edition of the Tengyur compiled by Bu-ton Rinchen Drubpa, presumably either because no Sanskrit edition was known in Bu-ton's time or else because Buton doubted the authenticity of the authorship. However, it was included in the Dergey Tengyur, and here I have translated it from that source.[2]

As mentioned in the Introduction, there are traditions of speaking about two, three, four, six, eight and ten yogas of Naropa. All ten are subsumed under the list of six. The more expansive arrangement simply separates out the various practices for the sake of convenience. When they become arranged as ten the list is as follows: (1) the generation stage yogas; (2) the view of emptiness; (3) the inner heat yoga; (4) karmamudra yoga; (5) the illusory body practice; (6) the clear light; (7) dream yoga; (8) the bardo yogas; (9) consciousness transference; and (10) forceful projection.[3] Naropa's text has verses that mention all ten of these, but places numbers two and four from the above list as doctrines eight and nine.

To facilitate an understanding of how he presents all ten in his short text I have provided the translation with subheads.

Vajra Verses of the Whispered Tradition

by the Indian Mahasiddha Naropa

Homage to the transcended and accomplished Buddha Vajradhara.

Eh-ma-hoh!
The supremely perfect teaching of all the buddhas,
The path of the supreme drop of victorious wisdom,
Is a reality beyond the expression of words.
But I once heard these words[4] of that great unborn path:
"I, Vajradhara, will speak of that auspicious meaning.
Offer homage, O Jnana Dakini, and listen well."

THE QUALIFICATIONS OF THE GURU AND THE DISCIPLE

The supreme guru is someone who is
Drunk with the experience of the three higher trainings.
The qualified disciple is someone who has
Confidence, energy, intelligence and compassion,
Is mindful of the shortcomings of worldly life
And has transcended all worldly concerns.

INITIATION AND THE GENERATION STAGE YOGAS

In the beginning one should rely upon the Chakrasamvara
    tantric tradition
By gaining the four initiations into the sixty-two deity mandala;

Perhaps also receive the four initiations of the fifteen dakinis.
Ripen the mind in this way, and practice wisdom and method
    combined.
Strive in the seven yogas, such as those like a king and minister;
Blending all as one taste, apply yourself to the three *samaya*.[5]

INNER HEAT YOGA

The pillar of the path is the self-blazing of the blissful inner heat.
With the bodily posture observing seven points, meditate
On the form of the deity, the body like an empty shell.
Envision the central channel avadhuti, the side channels lalana
    and rasana,
And also the four chakras, the syllables *AH* and *HAM*,
The blazing [of the inner fire] and dripping [of the drops],
And the entering of the life-sustaining and downward-moving
    energies
[Into the central channel].
Meditate on the vajra recitation with the five root energies.

Retain and stabilize [the energies], and induce the experience of wisdom.
Integrate the four blisses and blend the root energies and the drops.
Energy and consciousness enter into the central channel avadhuti;
The beyond-conceptuality mind arises, distorted emotions are
    self-pacified,
And an unbroken stream of bliss and radiance flows forth.

ILLUSORY BODY YOGA

See the nature of and remain absorbed in the sphere of Dharmakaya.
To intensify this awareness, meditate on the illusory, self-liberated
    nature of the eight worldly concerns.
See all things in samsara and nirvana as illusions;
They are illusory, like a rainbow and like the moon's reflection in water.

These functional phenomena that appear to the mind:
If they are as real and static as they seem, how could change occur?
But because they are deceptive forms, in essence they are unreal.
See all forms as empty appearances, like the echo in a cave.
Grasping at duality subsides, and one is freed from attraction and
    aversion.
With the basis of that insight, all actions become free from clinging
And one moves toward achieving the rainbow body and Dharmakaya.

DREAM YOGA

At night, strive to invoke the self-purification of confused dreams;
Guard the three doors with the hook of mindfulness.
Retain, purify, increase and transform the contents of dreams,
And eliminate all obstacles to the practice.
One rides on the sun and moon, travels to all buddhafields,
And behold! All "good" and "bad" illusions become self-liberated.

CLEAR LIGHT YOGA

Eventually to outshine the tenth stage and achieve the great purpose,
And especially, to separate the clear light from the darkness of
 ignorance,
Cultivate the yogic methods and engage in the four samadhis;
And behold! The sacred drop no longer is held by the three psychic
 poisons.
One holds to the place between sleep and the conceptual dream
 state, and
Integrates the four stages and the blendings of both day and night
 practice.
An inexpressible and unhindered experience of clear light arises,
 which is
The innate wisdom free from grasping at luminosity and emptiness.
One trains in this beyond-conceptuality mind
And beholds the Great Mahamudra itself.

CONSCIOUSNESS TRANSFERENCE YOGA

In the gold-maker method of consciousness transference,
By which buddhahood is achieved without meditation,
Wait for the signs of death to occur, and then
Place the mind in a state of joy and non-grasping.
Close the nine passageways, apply the tantric substances,
And adorn the practice with spiritual aspirations.
Energy and mind are brought together with *HUM* in avadhuti,
The mantra *KSHA* radiates; [mind] is thrown out of the body
Via the path of the brahma aperture, and is
Projected to the guru's Dharmakaya and then to a buddhafield.

FORCEFUL PROJECTION YOGA

Especially, in the practice of forceful projection into another residence,
Wherein one changes one's body like a snake shedding its skin,

Take control of energies and mind,
Make firm the generation and completion stage yogas, and
Throw consciousness in the form of a mantric syllable
Into a corpse that is free from faults.
For [both] these "transference" methods the yogi must know well
The time, place, substances required, and principles involved.

KARMAMUDRA YOGA

The practitioner who is free from doubts and who wishes
To engage in vast activities for the benefit of the world
Should seek the great bliss which is the secret of the dakinis.
He should rely on a mudra who is between
The ages of sixteen and twenty-five,
A diamond-like yogini qualified for the tantric sexual practices,
Such as the lotus-like, antelope-like, or conch-shell-like.
That fortunate practitioner, who is as though a Heruka Chakrasamvara,
Should, without grasping at duality, seek her sexual embrace
And sport in both worldly and beyond-worldly delight.

The drop that descends is to be retained, reversed,
And diffused to the appropriate sites.
This diffusion is to be done pervasively:
An eagle drinking the essence,
Like a lion, elephant, peacock, tiger and turtle.
And behold! Three aspects of the four blisses appear, making twelve.

The innate wisdom of inseparable nature is revealed,
And whatever occurs arises as non-worldly great bliss.
The secret initiation, mudra, nectar, pills:
Half of half of sixteen drops means four are given.
Bliss spreads through the four chakras and three channels.

If the yogi is drunk with mindlessness and attachment,
He misses the essence and falls to the realms of misery;
But if he applies the yogic techniques well,
Undoubtedly he will achieve buddhahood in this lifetime.

YOGA OF CULTIVATING THE VIEW

In order to ignite the radiance of Mahamudra wisdom,
Keep the three doors unmoving and tie the five senses well.
See without seeing; look at the nature of the mind.
Place the mind in its own place, unfabricated and without an object.

Not looking outside, realize the nature of the mind,
From its basis unfabricated, from the beginning spontaneous.
Place it in the great tradition of ordinary being;
Without movement it comes to see the immense sky
Of the unborn and undying Dharmakaya body.

However many phenomena appear as outer objects,
They are but one's own mind and have no other existence,
No matter what distortions, concepts, and graspings at duality
    manifest.
And behold! These things fade away of their own course.

The mind's essence is birthlessness, emptiness, Dharmakaya.
The unceasing radiant presences that arise are Nirmanakaya.
The non-abiding great bliss of integration is Sambhogakaya.
This is the meaning of Mahamudra, or [in Tibetan] *chak-gya chenpo*.
Here *chak* refers to all things being seen with the wisdom of non-duality;
Gya refers to the bliss of thus releasing the knots of cyclic behavior;
And *chenpo* means that it is the self-liberated Dharmakaya born
From the lamp of perfect integration, and not from something less.

The two obscurations are self-liberated; subject and object no longer
    polarized.
The discriminating mind, and all things in samsara and nirvana, fade.
The measure of knowledge is self-fulfilled with all good qualities
And one becomes a self-born buddha, beyond thought and words.

BARDO YOGAS

The profound meaning of the introduction to the bardo is revealed
And cuts off the three bardos:
The bardo of birth-to-death, the bardo of dreams, and the bardo of
    becoming.
Without giving there is giving; without seeing there is supreme seeing.
This is the radiant, empty self-awareness mind that is beyond
    conceptuality and is free from all obscurations,
Great bliss, the sphere of reality, utterly pure wisdom,
By nature indivisibly manifest as the three kayas. Behold!

Unrealized beings who practice with the three bardos should blend
The generation stage yogas, illusory body yoga, clear light yoga
    and Dharmakaya.
The elements—earth, water, fire and air—gradually dissolve;
The eighty conceptual minds are arrested, and three visions pass.

The white element, the red element, and mind itself collect into
   the lotus.
When this occurs, behold the face of the clear light mind;
Blend mother and child [clear lights] into inseparability.

THE RESULTS OF PRACTICE

The best trainees on the path of Dharmakaya buddhahood
Achieve enlightenment in this lifetime through these yogas.
Intermediate trainees achieve realization in the bardo.
Like a fish in water, they work Sambhogakaya transformations.
Five dances, five lights, three poisons, karmic forces,
Attachment and aversion: when moving toward rebirth
They apply the five blendings and take all as the path.
For those previously trained in the four mudras,
The bardo of becoming is the place for self-liberation.

Lesser trainees become free from attachment and aversion
And achieve an emanation body rebirth.
Using the general instructions, they eliminate hindrances
And recognize the host of maras.
They engage in the various vajra body exercises,
Such as the six roots yantras with thirty-nine branches,
And use every activity as a source of the accumulations.

If one can accomplish these stages of practice without mistake,
In four moments three joys are revealed.
Pure drops shower from above and arise from below;
The knots in the chakras are released,
And the vital energies enter the central channel.
Vital energies and emotional distortions—21,600 and five roots—
Are arrested and primordial wisdom arises.

From Pullimaru on up, the twenty-four sites and near-sites
Are made full; teachings come from the mouth of a perfect
   Nirmanakaya or Sambhogakaya,
A hundred clairvoyances are achieved, and one finds a treasure vase.
In one lifetime one traverses the stages of the enlightenment path
And attains the state of a Buddha Vajradhara.

For thirteen generations this teaching
Should be sealed in secrecy as an oral transmission.
It is the essence of all sutras and tantras
And brings liberation to the fortunate.
Use it to accomplish the meaningful.

The colophon: Thus is complete *The Vajra Verses: An Instruction to Jnana Dakini.* It is from the mouth of the Indian sage Mahapandita Naropa, and was translated [into Tibetan] and then ascertained by the translator Marpa Chokyi Lotru at the holy site known as Pushpahari.

3

Notes on
A Book of Three Inspirations

Tib. *Yid ches gsum ldan gyi bshad lung zin bris*

by

Jey Sherab Gyatso
1803–1875

Translator's Preamble

The longer of Lama Tsongkhapa's two treatises on the Six Yogas of Naropa, *A Book of Three Inspirations*, has served as the most popular Gelukpa teaching tool for public discourses on the Naropa tradition. It touches upon everything the practitioner wishing to engage in the Six Yogas should know, from the basic General Mahayana preliminary trainings, the special tantric preliminaries, what tantric initiations are necessary and why, and the preparatory generation stage yogas, up to the various techniques involved in the Six Yogas themselves.

In 1836 Jey Sherab Gyatso gave a public reading of *A Book of Three Inspirations*, and one of his students took notes on the discourse. After Jey Sherab Gyatso passed away these were published in his Collected Works.

Jey Sherab Gyatso's discourse mostly focuses on the preliminary trainings that someone wishing to enter into practice of the Six Yogas has to complete before entering into the actual trainings, and also on the special characteristics of the approach to emptiness associated with the Six Yogas tradition. We saw Naropa's verses on these subjects in the previous chapter; here Sherab Gyatso looks at some of the developments of this trend in Tibet.

The aim of Jey Sherab Gyatso's *Notes* is not to expand upon Tsongkhapa's treatise, but rather to contextualize some of the ideas found there. It thus works well as an introduction to the present volume in particular, and to the spiritual sentiment of the Six Yogas tradition in general. It is less technical in style than are the other works included in this volume because it was drawn from an oral discourse. In compiling the text the editors left out anything that they felt was perfectly clear in Tsongkhapa's writings and emphasized remarks made by Jey Sherab Gyatso during his discourse that they felt contributed to an understanding of little-known or controversial points in the training. The result is a gem of a text that sketches a skeletal portrait of the tradition.

Jey Sherab Gyatso was one of the preeminent Gelukpa masters of the nineteenth century. His many teaching activities as well as his numerous writings greatly contributed to the tremendous vibrancy that the Gelukpa achieved in that era.

In this text Jey Sherab Gyatso tells how he collected the transmission lineages of both of Lama Jey Tsongkhapa's texts on the Six Yogas—his formal treatise, *A Book of Three Inspirations*, and the shorter work found in his Collected Works, *A Practice Manual on the Six Yogas*. Although Jey Sherab Gyatso's *Notes* is a commentary to the longer of Tsongkhapa's two texts on the Six Yogas, it serves well as an introductory reader for his shorter manual, which is included as Chapter Five of the present volume. It also provides an excellent overview of the traditional approach to the Six Yogas trainings. In addition, his comments on the lineage of transmission and on various philosophical implications of the tradition throw light on the legacy of the Six Yogas tradition as maintained in the various Tibetan schools.

Notes on A Book of Three Inspirations

by Jey Sherab Gyatso

Marpa of Lodrak received numerous transmissions directly from the illustrious [Indian] pandit Naropa. Among these were six instructions drawn from the various tantric traditions. He gathered these six into the structure that has become famed as Naropa's Six Yogas. Each of these six contains a comprehensive presentation of the completion stage yogas, and the six as presented here provide a comprehensive approach to the completion stage yogas.

Naropa imparted the Six Yogas to Marpa, together with *The Vajra Song on the Six Yogas*. However, even though all six of these Dharmas certainly existed in India prior to Naropa, whether or not they had at that time been arranged into that structure is a point of doubt.

Naropa's Six Yogas was the unique instruction of the early Kargyu lamas. Lama Tsongkhapa the Great received this tradition, and later composed his treatise on the system, *A Book of Three Inspirations*. Thus the Six Yogas came into the Ganden [i.e., Geluk] order.

The Kargyupas are especially renowned for their tradition of the Six Yogas, and their early lineage masters, such as Marpa, Milarepa, Gampopa, Pakmo Drupa and Drikungpa Jigten Sumgon, were flawless elucidators of the tradition. However, as the lineage passed from generation to generation a large number of subtle points of unclarity found their way into many of the oral transmissions. Jey Gyalwa Nyipa [the Second Buddha, i.e., Tsongkhapa] removed these, and clarified all the key points and basic principles of the system. For this reason the lineage of the Six Yogas of Naropa as practiced within the Geluk order today is especially powerful.

I received the transmission of Tsongkhapa the Great's *A Book of Three Inspirations* from the great guru Drakkar Kachu Rinpochey[1] and trained in the yogas under him. At that time I was not able to receive the transmission of [the shorter text on the Six Yogas in Tsongkhapa's *Collected Works*, namely,] the notes on the Six Yogas made by Jangsem Kunzangpa[2] from Tsongkhapa's oral teachings. At that time my own tantric teacher had to leave the area, and I myself was quite busy, so was unable to request it from him. However, shortly thereafter Pa Rinto Yontsang had to go to Central Tibet, so I requested him to collect the lineage [of that text] from Gyalsey Rinpochey and to pass it to me on his return.[3] I had previously received instruction on the energy control and inner heat yogas, which had opened my eyes to these techniques; but these two texts by Tsongkhapa seemed to me to be unsurpassed in clarity on the subject. To have the opportunity to hear them is a most wondrous ripening of positive karma, and one should pay heed.

A widely used text for explaining the Six Yogas in other sects [prior to the time of Tsongkhapa the Great] was that known as *A Thousand Blazing Sunbeams*.[4] However, that manual is not particularly clear on the inner heat yoga, the physical exercises for purification, nor the meditations on the body as an empty shell. Moreover, many of the later Kargyu lamas had begun to by-pass the trainings in the General Mahayana as a preliminary to entering into tantric training, and had begun to teach the second stage of tantric practice [to which the Six Yogas of Naropa belong] without first establishing the basics of the first stage. Tsongkhapa composed *A Book of Three Inspirations* as a remedy to these problems.

To demonstrate the necessity of training in the General Mahayana meditations as a preliminary to tantric practice, Tsongkhapa quotes many of the early great Kargyu masters, such as Marpa, Milarepa, and so forth. In this way he demonstrates that the early Kargyu lamas did not condone by-passing the General Mahayana trainings.

As he points out, one should begin by making firm one's sense of spiritual refuge and one's maturity in the bodhisattva trainings [i.e., the General Mahayana teachings], and then receive the tantric empowerments.

To accomplish stability in these basic trainings, the early Kargyu masters advocated the preliminaries known as the "Four Dharmas of Dakpo Gampopa" (Tib. *Dvags po sGam po pa'i chos bzhis*): (1) meditations that cause the mind to turn toward the Dharma; (2) meditations that cause the Dharma to transform into the path; (3) meditations that cause the path to pacify confusion; and (4) meditations that cause confusion to arise as wisdom.[5]

Prior to Tsongkhapa the Great, Kargyu masters such as Yang Gonpa relied upon the meditative tradition embodied in the text *Twenty-One Instructions*, which contains ideas and practices similar to those found in the Lamrim literature and *Fifty Verses on the Guru*. Tsongkhapa advocates the Lamrim tradition of the master Atisha as the basis of the trainings in the General Mahayana practices; in *A Book of Three Inspirations* he refers to Atisha, and then quotes several verses from a song by Milarepa, in order to dispel the assumption, held by many, that the views of Atisha and Milarepa were in conflict on the subject of the need for the General Mahayana preliminaries.[6]

Milarepa's three verses embody the three levels of the Lamrim trainings: the first points to the initial level trainings, the second points to the intermediate trainings, and the remaining one points to the trainings of great perspective.

> If one does not contemplate the nature of karmic law—
> How positive and negative deeds produce concordant results—
> The subtle power of the ripening nature of activity
> May bring a rebirth of unbearable suffering.
> Cultivate mindfulness of action and its result.
>
> If one does not observe the faults of sensual indulgence
> And from within oneself reverse grasping at sensual objects,
> One will not become freed from the prison of samsara.
> Cultivate the mind that sees all as an illusion
> And apply an antidote to the source of suffering.
>
> If one is unable to repay the kindness of every living being
> Of the six realms, who has been one's own kind parent,
> One falls into the limitations of a narrow way.
> Therefore cultivate the universal bodhimind
> That looks on all beings with great concern and caring.

Milarepa's songs embody many doctrines unique to the Kargyu school, but most of them are in harmony with the teachings of Lama Tsongkhapa.

Lama Tsongkhapa quotes two more verses that similarly reflect how Milarepa's teachings were in accord with Atisha's doctrine of cultivating the three levels of spiritual perspective as a preliminary to tantric training.

> I experienced fear at the thought of the eight bondages
> And meditated on the shortcomings of impermanent samsara.
> Thus I settled my mind on the objects of spiritual refuge
> And learned to observe the laws of karmic cause and effect.
>
> I trained my spirit in method, which is the bodhimind,
> And cut off the stream of negative instincts and obscurations.
> I learned to see whatever appears as mere illusions,
> And thus no longer need fear the lower realms of misery.

Tsongkhapa thus speaks of the need for training the mind in the General Mahayana as a preliminary to entering into tantric training; and also of the need for then receiving the tantric empowerments as well as maintaining the disciplines and guidelines of tantric practice. He points out that a partial empowerment, and also a blessing empowerment, is not sufficient if one has not previously received the four complete initiations into an appropriate mandala system.

Some of the other schools [of Tibetan Buddhism], such as the Nyingma and Sakya, rely upon a cycle of texts known as "The Four Great Treatises on the Preliminary Practices" (Tib. *sNgon 'gro khrid chen bzhi*). Although there is nothing directly from the hand of Tsongkhapa the Great that deals with the preliminaries in that manner, i.e., with the General Mahayana and exclusive Vajrayana preliminaries in one text, he has written extensively on the General Mahayana preliminaries [in his Lamrim treatises] and treated those of the Vajrayana in various of his tantric works.

The two exclusive preliminaries emphasized in the Six Yogas system are those of Vajrasattva and guru yoga.[7] Both of these use some form of the seven-limbed rite. Actually, from within the range of practices for purifying the mind that are common to both the General Mahayana and the Vajrayana is that known as the seven-limbed rite, together with the mandala offering.[8] Furthermore, as a means of facilitating the guarding of the Vajrayana disciplines and guidelines, the Vajrasattva meditation and recitation of the hundred-syllable mantra is recommended. And even though some manuals on the tantric trainings state that the Vajrasattva practice is unnecessary for those who keep their disciplines well, nonetheless every school and sect that maintains a tradition of the Six Yogas of Naropa recommends it. As well, it is used in conjunction with almost all tantric systems of completion stage yoga.

In the meditation and mantra recitation of Vajrasattva, the way in which Vajrasattva is seen as an embodiment of all objects of refuge is common to all tantric deity-yoga practices. Here the tantric activity is that of purification of negative karma and spiritual obscurations, and hence there is a predominance of the color white in the meditation. For example, either the five buddhas who are summoned and hold up vases of empowering nectars are seen as being white in color, or else they emanate white lights; or else the five buddhas, four consorts and so forth of the complete mandala emphasize the color white.

In the meditation on guru yoga, the guru is visualized as appearing in the space in front of oneself in the form of Buddha Vajradhara, seated upon a throne upheld by eight lions. Whatever generation-stage mandala yoga one is engaged in, it is important always to see the mandala deities as being in the nature of one's guru; this leads to quick attainment of blessing powers. One's personal guru is more kind to one than are all the buddhas, for it is with him that one has karmic connections, and he whom one can see and hear directly. We have the link to communicate with him as directly as we do with our own parents.

Thus to visualize Buddha Vajradhara as above or separate from one's own guru is a mistaken mode of practice. This is not only the case in the guru yoga preliminary meditation, but also with all mandala deity-yoga practices. In the process of arising as the mandala deity, one should meditate that one's body and the body of the guru are of one inseparable nature, and that this arises in the form of the mandala deity. Similarly, one's speech is inseparably one with the speech of the guru, and this arises as the communicative power of the mandala deity. Third, one's mind is inseparably of one nature with that of the guru, and this arises as the mind of the mandala deity. Finally, one's suchness nature and that of the guru are inseparable, and this manifests as the suchness of the mandala deity.

When one meditates on the mandala deity in conjunction with guru yoga in this way, the siddhis are more quickly achieved.

The guru yoga meditation generally includes the symbolic offering of the universe in the form of a cosmogram. This is known as the mandala offering. When this is done in connection with completion stage yoga, the twenty-three part mandala offering is used [as opposed to the shorter seven-part or longer thirty-seven part mandala offerings]. The liturgy for the twenty-three part mandala offering was actually composed by Panchen Naropa himself [so it is especially relevant to the Six Yogas tradition].

One takes a mandala offering base and imagines that upon it one places the world and its inhabitants as offerings, together with the body, speech, mind, and pleasures of oneself and all others, from now until enlightenment is attained, and the root of goodness of times past, present, and future. All of this is offered as a mandala, visualized as having the nature of wisdom and precious gems, and presented in the manner of the bodhisattva Samantabhadra's peerless offerings, immeasurable in number as the extent of space. The master Tang Sakpa mentions this in his commentary to the Vajrabhairava mandala meditation. The tradition is not clear elsewhere, but is lucidly presented in *A Book of Three Inspirations*. The mandala offering is made in this way, and then the guru yoga meditation concludes with the four empowerments being bestowed by means of flowing nectars. The first three purify coarse karmic stains and obscurations collected by means of body, speech, and mind, and establish the seeds of the three buddha kayas.[9] The fourth empowerment purifies the subtle obscurations to omniscience and establishes the seed of *yuganaddha*, the state of great union. This is a specialty of the meditation as performed in the tradition of the Six Yogas of Naropa.

After these preliminary meditations for training the mind [through the General Mahayana meditations], purification [through Vajrasattva], and the enhancement of creative energy [through the meditation of guru yoga] have been made stable, one engages in the generation stage yogas.

The principle behind the generation stage yogas is the process known as "taking birth, death, and bardo as the path of the three kayas." The concept here is that by means of the generation stage yogas [the trainee] is introduced to the process of transforming the experiences of birth, death, and bardo into the three kayas of enlightenment: Dharmakaya, Sambhogakaya and Nirmanakaya. This prepares the mind for the methods of the completion stage yogas, which bring about this actual transformation.

The Sakya and Kargyu schools mostly rely upon simplified mandalas using only a pair of central deities, male-female-in-union, such as Hevajra and his consort Nairatmya, for accomplishing this

ripening process of the generation stage. However, Tsongkhapa recommends that in the beginning we should practice with a complete
mandala, and then later, when stability has been attained, reduce it to
the central male-female-in-union deity. This reduces the risk of incur-
ring dangerous side-effects from the yogas of working with the chakras,
energies, and so forth. It is not recommended to do the simplified deity practice from the beginning. The important principle here is that
the meditation upon the supporting mandala purifies perception of
the world, and meditation upon the supported mandala deities purifies the practitioner's five psychophysical aggregates.

This can be accomplished by meditation upon any of a number of
mandalas, but the mandala should be at least as complex as that of the
Ghantapada lineage of the Chakrasamvara mandala, which has five
deities, for we want to purify the five psychophysical aggregates and
transform the five inner distortions into the five wisdoms.

An exception to this rule [of a mandala having a minimum of five
deities], as Tsongkhapa points out in several of his writings, is the
mandala of Solitary Vajrabhairava, wherein a single mandala deity
suffices for the process. Many lamas from other schools question
Tsongkhapa's logic on this recommendation of Solitary Vajrabhairava.
Tsongkhapa's idea here is that the Vajrabhairava mandala combines
elements from both the male and female tantric cycles and is unique
in this respect.

In fact, Tsongkhapa held the view that because Naropa's Six Yogas
embodies elements from both the male and female tantras, it is ac-
ceptable to prepare for training in the Six Yogas by practicing the generation stage yogas with any of the three main tantric cycles: Guhyasamaja, Heruka Chakrasamvara, or Vajrabhairava. Tsongkhapa points
out that many of the early gurus used either Hevajra or Heruka
Chakrasamvara as their personal meditational deity, and thus they
accomplished the generation stage yogas in conjunction with a
mandala from one of those two cycles. However, this does not mean
that the practitioner is limited to these two mandala cycles.

The process of the generation stage yogas begins by concentrating
on oneself as the lord of the mandala surrounded by the mandala entourage. If the central deity has many faces and hands, one first concentrates on the main face and accomplishes clarity with it. One then concentrates on the two main hands. After that one gradually supplements

the visualization with other details of the main deity, and then goes on to the consort, entourage, and supporting mandala, until all appears with total clarity.

In conjunction with this practice of cultivating radiant visualization of the mandala and its deities one cultivates the divine pride, "I am the tantric deity." At first this thought is contrived, but gradually it arises spontaneously.

On the generation stage of practice the divine tantric pride of having the form of the deity is accomplished. Then during the completion stage yoga, at the phase of practice known as "the vajra recitation," the divine tantric pride of the communicative dimension of the deity is accomplished. Finally, the divine tantric pride of the mind of the deity is accomplished at the stage of the clear light yogas.

After the generation stage yogas have been made firm one engages in the cultivation of the view of emptiness.

These days in Tibet there are many lamas who teach that the emptiness philosophy of the tantras is different from that of Arya Nagarjuna, and that the former is higher. However, many different sources, including the collection of texts known as "Four Interwoven Treatises" (Tib. *'Grel pa bzhi sbrags*), reveal how the two systems are in harmony.

Some Kargyupas even say that the Mahamudra philosophy of Marpa and Milarepa is higher than the Madhyamaka emptiness doctrine of Nagarjuna. Tsongkhapa quotes a song by Lama Marpa to show that the two—Madhyamaka and Mahamudra—are in harmony:

> I travelled to the banks of the Ganges River
> And there, through the kindness of Guru Maitripa,
> Realized the uncreated nature of phenomena.
> I seized with my bare hands the emptiness nature of
>   my own mind,
> Beheld the primordial essence beyond concepts,
> Directly encountered the mother of the three kayas,
> And severed the net of my confusion.

This demonstrates how Marpa achieved his understanding of Mahamudra under Maitripa. This master was definitely a follower of Chandrakirti, the great elucidator of Nagarjuna's Madhyamaka doctrine of emptiness, as demonstrated by [Maitripa's treatise] *Ten Reflections on Simple Suchness*. Tsongkhapa quotes this text,

> If you wish to experience the quintessential nature of being [i.e., voidness], be aware that it is not with characteristics and not without characteristics.

His point in using this passage is that it proves Maitripa was definitely a proponent of the Prasangika Madhyamaka view. Maitripa is saying that the approach to emptiness philosophy as presented by the two Svatantrika Madhyamaka schools—that advocating "emptiness with characteristics" and that advocating "emptiness without characteristics"—do not have the capacity to induce the final wisdom of suchness, so how much more is this the case with the lower schools, such as Vaibashika, Sautrantika and Yogachara, which speak in terms of "true aspects" and "false aspects"?

Then, in order to show that this is not merely his personal interpretation of Maitripa's words, Tsongkhapa quotes an Indian commentary to the passage. This commentary was written by Sahajavajra, a direct disciple of Maitripa. Tsongkhapa states,

> The mahasiddha Maitripa's direct disciple, the pandit Sahajavajra, explains that in the scriptures of the Shravakas we see a discussion of "emptiness with characteristics," as is popular with the Sautrantika school of [Indian Buddhist] thought; and "emptiness without characteristics," as is popular with the Vaibashika school. Moreover, he continues, in the [Mahayana schools such as] the Yogachara, we see a discussion of emptiness having "true and false characteristics," and in the Yogachara Madhyamaka school the doctrine of "conventionally true characteristics and conventionally false characteristics." ...One should rely upon the approach to emptiness elucidated by the great Madhyamaka masters Arya Nagarjuna, Aryadeva, Chandrakirti, and so forth, who teach that the interdependent, co-existent nature of phenomena points to the suchness of being. We should adopt the guidelines set forth by these three masters.

This passage demonstrates unquestionably that Maitripa, under whom Marpa achieved his realization of Mahamudra, was a master in the Prasangika Madhyamaka lineage.

Tsongkhapa then again quotes [Maitripa's] *Ten Reflections on Simple Suchness,*

> To put it plainly, most of these gurus are merely
> Unadorned, mediocre teachers of the Middle View.

Maitripa's point here is that most Madhyamaka teachers are not adorned with the oral tradition teachings from Chandrakirti and therefore are but mediocre proponents of the Middle View. By "mediocre" he means that they have not achieved the Prasangika understanding and rely upon less exalted lineages of the emptiness doctrine, such as those of the various Svatantrika schools.

The Prasangika understanding of emptiness, as re-expressed in the Mahamudra teachings of Marpa, provides the most excellent platform from which the tantric yogas, such as inner heat yoga, energy control and so forth, can be accomplished.

In Tsongkhapa's time, however, most Tibetan schools had lost the philosophical subtlety of the emptiness doctrine as taught by Chandrakirti and Maitripa. Many of them took the expressions "not true and not false" to mean that one should engage in a blank-minded meditation in the pursuit of the wisdom of emptiness.

To show the correct meaning of these terms Tsongkhapa quotes Nagarjuna's *Sixty Stanzas on Emptiness:*

> All the various objects of experience
> Are like the moon's reflection in water;
> Neither really true nor really false.
> Those appreciating this do not lose the view.

Tsongkhapa then states,

> One should understand the emptiness doctrine in the context of this simile. The wise perceive that all things—persons and phe-nomena—arise in reliance upon their own causes and conditions, and that based on this process we impute mental labels upon things. The phenomena themselves have no true or inherent ex-istence from their own side. They have no self-nature whatsoever.

In other words, the expression "not really true" means that on the ultimate level of reality they have no final or findable existence, no inherent self-existence. The expression "not really false" means that on the conventional level of reality they nonetheless function and seem to exist. To the ordinary mind, they seem to exist and function as though being real.

Next Tsongkhapa quotes Milarepa, Marpa's chief disciple, to dem-onstrate how Milarepa upheld this same view,

> For those of weaker minds the omniscient Buddha taught,
> To accord with the predispositions of those to be trained,
> That the objects of knowledge have real existence;
> But from the perspective of higher truth, nothing
> From a hindering spirit to a buddha has real existence.

> There are no meditators, no objects of meditation,
> No spiritual progress, no path with signs,
> No resultant kayas, no wisdom,
> And therefore no nirvana.

Solely by means of names and mental labels
The stable and moving elements of the three worlds
Are established; in reality from the very beginning
They are unproduced, uncreated, baseless, and innately unborn.

There is no karma nor ripening effects of actions,
And therefore even the name "samsara" does not exist.
This is the sense of the final truth.

Elsewhere Milarepa states,

Eh-ma! If there are no living beings, how then
Can the buddhas of the three times come into being?
Without a cause, there will be no effect.

From the perspective of conventional reality,
All things in samsara and nirvana,
Which the Buddha has accepted as conventionally valid,
All existents, things, appearances, non-existents,
All these functional realities, are inseparably
Of one taste with the quintessential nature of emptiness.
There is no self-awareness and no other-awareness.
All share in the vastness of yuganaddha, the great union.

The wise who realize this truth
No longer see mind, but only wisdom-mind.
They no longer see living beings, only buddhas.
They no longer see phenomena, only the quintessential nature.

Here Milarepa is showing how the Buddha taught the conventional truth that things exist, to accord with the mindset and perception of ordinary beings, and the conventional validity of relative existence. However, Buddha also taught the relationship of the two truths such that phenomena are established as valid and capable of performing functions yet even conventionally they have no intrinsic self-nature. The ultimate truth of things is that they lack a findable self-nature. The conventional truth of things is that they exist validly, but not in the manner in which we perceive and conceive them; rather they exist as mental imputations and labels which nonetheless perform the functions of those objects. In this way the two truths co-exist as one entity.

This was the understanding of emptiness held by the early Kargyu masters, and it is in complete harmony with the understanding of Chandrakirti. So let's face it: If Marpa and Milarepa, the two great early Tibetan masters of the Six Yogas tradition, did not know the special features of the Mahamudra emptiness philosophy associated with the transmission, who does? As Tsongkhapa so eloquently suggests, to take the Mahamudra doctrine beyond what Marpa and Milarepa taught is to contradict the very basis of this Kargyupa legacy.

Some previous Mahamudra teachers have taught that in the practice of Mahamudra there is no need for a balance of the two levels of truth. Here the term "balance" is the same as that used for the keel[10] of a boat which keeps the boat straight and prevents it from tipping to the right or left. In the same way, just as a keel is required in order to ensure that a boat does not tip over to the right or left, a balance is required in meditation upon the two levels of truth in order to ensure that one does not fall into the extremes of reification or nihilism.

The treatment of the emptiness doctrine here falls under the discussion of the introduction to the nature of the mind. Three dimensions of the mind are mentioned: the coarse mind, which is constituted of the six sensory consciousnesses and so forth, and is easily understood; the more subtle level, which is constituted of the six primary *kleshas* and twenty secondary kleshas; and the most subtle, which is what is referred to in the expression "most subtle level of energy and consciousness." This third arises when the most subtle bodily energies have been isolated from the coarse energies. This most subtle consciousness, when placed in the vision of emptiness, renders the path most easily accomplished. It is the emptiness described by Nagarjuna that is the object of meditation of that most subtle consciousness.

The first of the Six Yogas is that of the inner heat yoga. Although in the inner heat yoga it is not totally inappropriate to focus exclusively upon one of the chakras, this approach is discouraged. The navel chakra is the main chakra with which one works, but the others are also important in the process.[11]

As a preliminary to the inner heat yoga one engages in various physical exercises, or yantras. There are a wide variety of these associated with the Six Yogas of Naropa, such as the set of six, the set of thirty-two, and so forth. The Pakmo Dru and Drikung sects of the Kargyu school both maintain a tradition of 108 exercises. Even though these are impressive and useful, there seems to be no great advantage in doing more than the six recommended by Pakmo Drupa [as taught in Tsongkhapa's treatise] for accomplishing the inner heat yogas.

The first of the six is the vase breathing exercise. Even though all of the remaining five are done within the sphere of this breathing technique, it nonetheless is counted as one of the six. These six exercises are regarded as a preliminary to the Six Yogas, and thus are not counted as a separate yoga.

In the exercise called "showing the mudra of vajra binding, lifting upward toward the sky, and then pressing downward," the head is held face upward. In all the others it is held downward [i.e., in the normal position]. Also, with the exception of the exercise called "straightening the body like an arrow and expelling the air like a dog heaving," in which the air is forcefully expelled through the mouth, in all the exercises the breath is made to pass exclusively through the nose.

The exercise "circling like a wheel" may be done in either of two ways: with the feet placed in front of the body and soles facing one another; or with legs crossed in the vajra posture. In either case one holds the two big toes. Similarly, the exercise that uses the mudra of vajra binding can be done with the palms facing up on the up-stretch and then facing down on the down-stretch, or can be done with arms crossed; there are these two ways. Also, the "heaving like a dog" exercise can be done in two ways: with the hands placed as in the meditation mudra, one above the other; or with them placed on the floor, as in the position of making a full-length prostration.

These exercises are followed by the meditation on the body like an empty shell. Here the body and the energy channels are to be seen as completely transparent and radiant.

If one enters into the completion stage yogas [such as the Six Yogas of Naropa] without first achieving great stability in these preliminary trainings, there is the danger that one will experience considerable physical pain as a result of the changing energy flows. To avoid this, one should do as many of the physical exercises as possible, in conjunction with the meditation on the body as an empty shell. When stability in these practices is achieved, one will experience a sense of subtle joy that pervades the body, and the possibility of pain arising in the body or mind will be eliminated. When progress in the practice comes without pain or hardship, this indicates that one is proceeding correctly.

In general it is said that the Six Yogas can be practiced in any of three ways: for achieving enlightenment in this lifetime; for achieving it in the bardo; and for achieving it over a series of lives. No matter which way is appropriate to oneself, one should begin the training now. The best practitioner will achieve enlightenment in this life; the intermediate will achieve it in the bardo; and the least will achieve it over a series of lives.

It is also said that the inner heat yoga and karmamudra yoga [i.e., sexual practices] are oral instructions emanating from the *Hevajra Tantra*; the illusory body yoga and clear light yoga are oral instructions emanating from the *Chakrasamvara Tantra* and *Guhyasamaja Tantra*; and the consciousness transference yoga and forceful projection yoga are oral instructions emanating from the *Shri Chaturpita Tantra*. Thus all six were originally taught by the Buddha.

In earlier days the dream yogas were not emphasized in the system of the Six Yogas of Naropa, and the yoga of forceful projection did not exist in the system of the Six Yogas of Niguma. It seems that this difference is the reason for maintaining these two [i.e., the Naropa and Niguma traditions of the Six Yogas] as separate systems. Otherwise, the two are very similar.[12]

The elaborative nature of the force of darkness causes confusion to increase in the minds of sentient beings. Because of the manner in which the darkness of confusion increases, the expression "darkness emanation" is used. The generation stage yogas, in which the radiant appearance of the mandala and its deities is emphasized, are therefore necessary as a preliminary to engaging in the Six Yogas.

The first of the six is the inner heat yoga, which is accomplished by meditation on the *AH*-stroke mantric syllable at the navel chakra. This yoga gives rise to the simultaneously born bliss, which in turn then acts as a simultaneously present condition for the practice of the sexual or karmamudra yogas. Therefore the expression "inner heat karmamudra" is used.

From within the Six Yogas, the principal methods used for accomplishing enlightenment in this lifetime are the illusory body and clear light yogas. In the beginning of the training the inner heat yoga, karmamudra yoga, and so forth, are utilized as methods for drawing the subtle physical energies into the central channel in order to induce the four blisses. These four blisses, and especially the simultaneously born bliss, are prerequisites for practicing the illusory body and clear light yogas. This principle is common to all completion stage yoga systems.

There is no single standard way of engaging in the inner heat yoga. For example, the size in which the energy channels are visualized varies in accordance with the capacities of trainees. Similarly, the chakra used as the site at which to draw the energies into the central channel varies. However, there is less danger of undesirable side-effects when one works with the chakra at the navel. Consequently the two side channels are generally visualized as curling into the mouth of the central channel at the site of the navel chakra. It is best first to establish control over the subtle energies at the navel chakra. Should one try to do this at any of the three upper chakras and apply the techniques forcefully, there is the danger that the upper energies will be disturbed and that negative side-effects will be produced, such as intense turbulence of the heart energies, and so forth. Similar dangers are associated with working with the secret chakra. There are numerous ways of visualizing the mantric syllables in the practice of the inner heat, as well as of retaining the energies and directing the inner heat that is induced.

The two most clear and concise manuals on the manner of meditating on the inner heat are those by [the Second Dalai Lama] Gyalwa Gendun Gyatso and [the First Panchen Lama] Panchen Chogyen.[13] One should meditate in accordance with their instructions, for they present the tradition embodied in Tsongkhapa's *A Book of Three Inspirations* in a most wonderful and practical manner.

It is very important that the mantric syllables at the chakras are seen as being inside the central channel. Many early Tibetan lamas overlooked this crucial principle. The smaller the syllables are visualized, the more easy it becomes to draw the energies into the central channel. The syllables should be seen as blazing with light, as this will eliminate the danger of mental dullness obstructing the meditation.

Of the five fundamental energies that are to be drawn into the central channel at the navel chakra, it is said that the all-pervading energy generally does not flow. The upward-rising and downward-expelling energies respectively have the nature of fire and water, and flow forcefully to the right and left. The life-sustaining and equalizing energies flow simultaneously and are of equal strength.

The vase breathing technique is used in the process of bringing these energies into the navel chakra. Generally one first draws in the airs from above, and then draws them up from below. An exception occurs after the energies have entered into the navel chakra and dissolved. At that time the lower energies are drawn in first. The vase breathing exercise is also said to be a supreme method for increasing health and longevity. It is best to practice it at the navel chakra. To do so at the heart or throat chakras is dangerous.

Tsongkhapa quotes a verse from *The Arising of Samvara Tantra*,

> The energies that course above and below
> Through the mind are brought to a kiss.

Here the expression "kiss" refers to the vital energies being dissolved into the *nada* above the mantric *AH*-stroke syllable at the navel chakra.

Accomplishment in the inner heat yoga brings about great spiritual power. Once when the yogi Paljor Rabten was drinking beer I asked him, "O great mahasiddha, what are you meditating upon?"

He replied, "On the *AH*-stroke mantra of the Six Yogas of Naropa."

I asked him, "And what benefits have you gotten out of it?"

"I achieved limitless, immeasurable realizations," he replied. "When I was in retreat on the Six Yogas at Lodrak Drowolung I received many visions of the five buddhas as well as many bodhisattvas. Then when I made retreat on the energy practices and inner heat yogas at Samyey Chimpu I received visions of the buddhas of the ten directions, and many more."

I once asked another yogi friend what he was meditating upon.

He replied, "On the inner heat yoga."

"Well then, you must be able to levitate," I said.

"I haven't dedicated myself to the meditation for doing that; but if I were to do so, no doubt I could," he replied. In fact, it was well known that he had achieved the power of levitation and flight.

Although I did not test the validity of their claims, meditating on the inner heat yogas definitely does bring about such experiences and abilities. For example, the yogi Milarepa was seen levitating through the air on numerous occasions.

On another occasion I met a seventy-year-old hermit at Palkor Chodey Monastery. I asked him, "O mahasiddha, what are you doing?"

He replied honestly, "If one takes up meditation early in life, there is no doubt that great realization can be achieved. But what can you expect from an old man like me? I am a disciple of Jetsun Lobzang Yeshey of Tashi Lhunpo Monastery. But I broke my vows and now live here in retreat."

His point was well taken. It is important to take up practice before old age has weakened one's body and mind, and also important to keep whatever spiritual precepts one has taken. Then realization is easily accomplished.

By means of the inner heat yoga the vital energies are drawn into the central channel. As said earlier, this technique is based on the oral instructions emanating from the *Hevajra Tantra*. What then follows is similar to the process as described in the "five stages" of the Guhyasamaja Tantra system, and the "four yogas" of the Vajrabhairava Tantra system. The knots constricting the chakra at the heart are loosened, and when they are released the illusory body is achieved. Thus the inner heat yoga is a method for facilitating practice of the illusory body.

The instructions on the illusory body and clear light yogas are presented with great clarity in Lama Marpa's oral tradition of the Guhyasamaja text known as *Elucidation of the Summary of the Five Stages*. These instructions are clearly explained in Tsongkhapa's works *A Clear Lamp on the Five Stages* and *The Complete Seat*.

However, even though the illusory body and clear light yogas as presented in the Six Yogas tradition are based on the *Heruka Chakra-samvara Tantra* and *Guhyasamaja Tantra*, the way in which they have been taught by earlier Tibetan lineage masters is mainly designed for beginners in tantric practice. Their central purpose is to establish karmic instincts for the real trainings.

These early lineage masters taught the illusory body training under three topics: the illusory nature of appearances; the illusory nature of dreams; and the illusory nature of the bardo experience.

Lama Tsongkhapa does not reject these practices as taught by the early lineage masters. However, he does point out in *A Book of Three Inspirations* that the techniques taught in the illusory body training, such as those classified as "seeing all that appears as an illusion" and "realizing dream illusions" are essentially for beginners, and only have the function of laying the karmic seeds for the real practice of the illusory body yoga. They suffice as meditations for beginners, but are not what he considers to be the actual illusory body trainings.

Seeing all that appears as an illusion involves two levels of trainings: unpurified, in which one meditates on the dream-like, illusory nature of the objects of experience; and purified, in which the illusory appearances are caused to arise as the mandala and its deities. In the second of these the main practice is conducted in a room with a window in each wall. One opens all the windows and arranges a mirror in front of a Vajrasattva image. One then places a bowl of water on the floor between the two, and arranges the mirror so that it projects the image of Vajrasattva into the bowl of water. One then contemplates this image, and just as in the generation stage practice, meditates that one arises as the mandala deity and that the image reflected in the water is the image of oneself as the deity. It is said that this practice was taught by both Marpa Lotsawa and Goe Lotsawa. One then blends this with the illusory nature meditations.

In the dream yoga section of *A Book of Three Inspirations* Tsongkhapa refers to a tantric scripture known as *The Advaya Vijaya Tantra*, which states that one may visualize the five mantric syllables *OM AH NU TA RA* standing at the throat chakra on a four-petalled lotus, with *OM* in the center and the remaining four syllables on the four petals. Alternatively, one may simply use a solitary syllable, either *OM* or *AH*, at the center, and dispense with the remaining four. The scripture comments that using the four extra syllables does not bring any added power to the practice.

Many Tibetan scholars question the authenticity of the above scripture. However, if it is inauthentic then the instruction is likewise inauthentic. There are numerous other sources for the dream yoga instruction, but this text is quite important. It would seem that if Tsongkhapa had confidence in it, it probably is reliable. Moreover, no solid logic for rejecting it has been forthcoming. Tsongkhapa regards *The Five Stages* and *The Four Seats* as the most important sources of the dream yoga teaching.

The dream yoga should be practiced in a solitary place. If one is unable to accomplish lucid dreaming at night, then one should attempt the practice between early dawn and sunrise. This will encourage especially clear dreams. As dreams are linked to the throat chakra, this is the chakra most commonly used in the training.

Should one find one's sleep to be too light, or if one repeatedly awakens, one should meditate on the mantric syllable [or syllables] as being less bright. When sleep is too heavy and as a result one cannot notice or clearly remember one's dreams, one should apply the methods called "cutting the obstacle of heaviness." Should sleep come but no dreams occur, one should apply the methods called "cutting the obstacle of nothingness." If sleep comes but one quickly awakens from it, one should apply the methods called "cutting the obstacle of awakening." These terms were used by the lineage masters of old. Tsongkhapa accepts them without reinterpretation or adaptation.

It is said that the inner heat yoga is the foundation stone of all Six Yogas. Thus it is also the foundation stone of dream yoga. Through the inner heat yoga one gains control over the vital energies of the body; one then applies this control when going to sleep in order to conduct the dream yoga practice. Dream yoga can also be engaged through the force of conscious resolution, yet this is not the primary method. The primary method is energy control born from the inner heat yoga. Conscious resolution is only intended as a supplement.

After stability in the practice of lucid dreaming has been established one takes up the dream practice known as "the illusory dream deeds." These are of two types: worldly and para-worldly. Both involve projecting one's dream body to special realms from within the dream state.

The difference between the two is the purity of the realms to which one projects oneself. The latter refers to projecting oneself to the buddhafields, such as Sukhavati and so forth.

By engaging in the technique of illusory dream deeds one projects oneself in the dream state to a buddhafield and meditates there. But is this a reliable experience? Can one really project oneself to a buddhafield?

If the technique is applied by means of energy control, and one has loosened the knots constricting the chakras to the point that the illusory body has almost been attained, then the experience is valid. For example, Lama Wonton Kyergangwa projected himself into the presence of Guru Padma Sambhava and received direct teachings on the Hayagriva Tantra. Nonetheless such instances are rare and their validity is difficult to ascertain.

With dream experiences that arise as a result of the technique being applied through energy control, it seems that sometimes they are clear and sometimes not, sometimes valid and sometimes not. When the method is conscious resolution, they usually are not valid. There are, however, methods for enhancing their reliability.

The first step in dream yoga is to learn to retain conscious presence during dreams. Later one meditates on the suchness of dreams. However, merely recognizing that the horses, elephants and so forth that are seen in dreams are illusions will not give rise to the wisdom of emptiness, in the same way that realizing something to be an illusion in the waking state, such as one's reflection in a mirror, does not give rise to realization of emptiness. One must combine the technique of dream yoga with the instructions on the methods of ascertaining the meaning of emptiness.

The third level of the illusory body yoga is the training in the illusory nature of the bardo.

Milarepa speaks of three bardos: the bardo of life, which occurs [in the waking state] between birth and death; the dream bardo, which occurs between going to sleep and waking up; and the bardo of becoming, which refers to the time between death and rebirth. Tsongkhapa explains these three concepts in depth in *A Book of Three Inspirations*.

The expression "blending desire with the non-contaminated" is used. Here "desire" refers to great bliss and "non-contaminated" refers to the wisdom of emptiness. One blends the wisdom of emptiness with the great bliss generated through bringing the energies into the central channel and then directing the drop through the chakras.

It is said that there is no bardo for those entering into the highest worldly realms, nor for those who have created any of the five most terrible karmic deeds. Those two types of beings take rebirth immediately after death, without experiencing the bardo.

As the death process sets in, a series of outer and inner signs occurs. The outer signs, such as losing control over bodily strength and so forth, can be witnessed by others. The inner signs, such as the visions of a mirage, smoke and so forth, can only be experienced by oneself. Eventually the inner sign of the clear light of death arises. This is the final stage, after which consciousness exits the body.

[The Second Dalai Lama's guru] Khedrup Norzang Gyatso stated,

> When the appearance of the clear light of death arises, the mind of duality relaxes and the mind of utter simplicity, as unfabricated as space, arises. This is the actual mind of the wisdom of emptiness, yet untrained beings will not recognize it as such. For the practitioner trained in the tantric yogas, this clear light of death becomes the experience of the mind experiencing emptiness. However, if one has not previously achieved realization of emptiness, there will be no realization now.

Thus Khedrup Norzang Gyatso refers to this consciousness of the clear light of death as "a consciousness which appears but is unrecognized by the experiencer." Even though his view here does not accord with that of Lama Jey Tsongkhapa, it is worth considering. He makes this statement in his commentary to the completion stage yogas of the Guhyasamaja system. I have not seen it said elsewhere.

An important element in the bardo practice is the wisdom of bliss and emptiness. For this, the bliss that is induced through bringing the vital energies into the central channel and directing the drop through the chakras is the "bliss" being referred to.

One lies in the "sleeping lion" posture, with one's head to the north and back to the east, and mind focused on the mantric syllable unmistakenly inside the central channel. One observes the natural dissolution of the elemental energies during the dying process, and the visions such as the mirage, smoke, and so forth. When the clear light of death appears one concentrates on it and simultaneously applies the techniques for ascertaining the wisdom of emptiness. However, if one has not previously achieved meditative samadhi, it will be difficult to recognize the clear light of death.

It is important to critically examine the teachings of Lama Tsongkhapa in order to plant the instincts of realization. In particular, three of his tantric works—*A Book of Three Inspirations, A Clear Lamp on the Five Stages,* and *The Complete Seat*—should be studied in conjunction with one another. Then an inconceivable understanding is produced. This is especially important in gaining profound appreciation of the illusory body and clear light doctrines.

The final two doctrines in the Six Yogas system, both of which are classified as branches of the path, are those of consciousness transference to a higher realm and forceful projection of one's consciousness from its present residence into the residence of another body. Both of these are forms of consciousness transference. The first is ordinary and the second is extraordinary. The former can be accomplished simply by means of firm conscious resolution; the latter can only be accomplished by means of the power induced through directing the subtle physical energies into the central channel.

The purpose of the yogas of consciousness transference and forceful projection is that some practitioners may apply themselves to the Six Yogas but still not accomplish enlightenment in this lifetime. They then utilize one of these two yogas at the time of death.

To apply either of these techniques prematurely is equivalent to suicide. As one is a tantric practitioner, and thus one's body is the residence of hundreds of tantric deities, it is equivalent to killing hundreds of tantric deities. Tsongkhapa states that this breaks the eighth tantric precept. However, Khedrup Norzang Gyatso questions him on this in his text *A Clear Lamp on the Precepts,* pointing out that, by the time the transference or forceful projection has been completed, the basis of that karma has already gone.

[The Second Dalai Lama's guru] Khedrup Norzang Gyatso questions Tsongkhapa's teachings on numerous points in this way. Langdol Lama criticizes Norzang Gyatso for this, saying that as he [Norzang] is a follower of Tsongkhapa it is not appropriate. Norzang Gyatso accepted Tsongkhapa's doctrines in general, but raised questions on many subtle points of doctrine.

As with the other doctrines, in the practice of consciousness transference the best application is that of using the inner heat yoga to bring the vital energies into the central channel and give rise to the great bliss and simultaneously born wisdom.

A number of mandala deities can be used as the basis of the transference yoga. Tsongkhapa's *A Commentary on Consciousness Transference Yoga* recommends the thirteen-deity mandala of Jnana Dakini. This system does not use the *AH-HIK* mantra at the time of training, as is done in the Six Yogas system. The *AH-HIK* is only used at the time of actual application of the yoga [i.e., at the time of death]. My own guru Drakkar Kachu Rinpochey taught that the *AH-HIK* is invoked because the *AH*-stroke mantric syllable at the lower region of the central channel must be made to move upward and strike against the *KSHA* syllable that blocks the upper aperture, thus removing it.

In the system of consciousness transference based on Buddha Amitabha, as practiced by Lubum Ritropa Lobzang Dondrub,[14] a master of the ten instructions, the *AH-HIK* syllable is used at the time of practice as well as at the time of actual application. Thus it seems to be the same as is taught in the Six Yogas. According to Kyabgon Dorjey Chang,[15] although the Buddha Amitabha system of consciousness transference essentially belongs to the *kriya* division of tantric practice, it is conjoined with the oral tradition teachings of highest yoga tantra. Essentially it is a method for transference of consciousness to a higher realm.

In general, if one has complete control over the movement of the vital energies, there is no need to visualize mantric syllables in order to block the gateways of the senses when the transference yogas are engaged. Otherwise, one should use them. [Tsongkhapa's] *A Commentary on Consciousness Transference Yoga* explains that there are a number of ways of utilizing [i.e., visualizing] the mantric syllables, as well as various mantras to be used. Panchen Tamchey Khyenpa[16] taught that simply placing a syllable *HUM* at the nine gateways is sufficient. Another tradition recommends that we use two syllables of *HUM*, with an *AH* syllable between the *U*-vowel [of the pair of *HUM* syllables]. Tsongkhapa does not mention this technique.

The second form of transference, that known as *drong-jug*, or "forceful projection to a new residence," involves one of two techniques: projecting one's consciousness out of one's body and into that of a corpse; or, alternatively, evacuating one's body and projecting the consciousness of someone else into it.

Here the word "residence" is used because the body is the residence of the senses. The source of the term is the Prajnaparamita literature. In particular, it comes from the passage in the *Prajnaparamita Sutra in 100,000 Verses* that begins with the lines,

> One wins the battle with the emotional afflictions
> And with the residence of the senses and sensory powers....

If one is to master the yogas of consciousness transference and forceful projection as taught exclusively in the tantric scriptures, one should begin by training in the General Mahayana meditations, taking the

tantric empowerments, guarding the disciplines and precepts, cultivating stability in the generation stage yogas, and then, by means of
the inner heat yogas, gaining the ability to bring the vital energies into
the central channel. The prerequisites demanded for successful practice of forceful projection to a new residence are even more intense
than those for mere transference to a higher realm.

In the forceful projection training one takes a human skull cup and
places it on a platform marked with the design of a mandala. The
skull can be placed like a cup, and a mantric syllable *HUM* written
inside of it with *do-gyu* (Tib. *rdo rgyu*) stone, or else the skull can be
reversed and the *HUM* written on top. One then engages in the training as instructed.

Before attempting to do the actual application it is important to test
oneself to be sure that one is ready. To do this one takes the corpse of
an animal and engages the technique with it as the object. If it warms
up, this is a sign that one is ready for the real application. One then
gets a fresh human corpse, such as that of a young child that has been
left for dead in a charnel ground. The projection is best accomplished
by someone who has complete mastery over the vital energies; however, lesser practitioners who have accomplished the generation stage
yogas can also accomplish it.

There is a tradition of vacating one's own body in order to offer it
as a residence to someone else. However, Tsongkhapa only mentions
this application, but doesn't describe it. That technique is similar to
the method of consciousness transference.

Finally, the tradition of the Six Yogas of Naropa speaks of special
activities and enhancement techniques for propelling one through tran-
sitional stages of the path. There are those of the generation stage associated with the accomplishment of the eight siddhis, or magical abilities, and the accomplishment of vast enlightenment deeds. Then on
the completion stage there are the three types of special activities
known as "with embellishment," "without embellishment," and "utterly without embellishment." There are also the special activities associated with the five ordinary paths. By relying upon these, one eventually is transported to the enlightenment state known as *yuganaddha*,
or complete integration.

The textual source of the Six Yogas tradition is the twofold collection known as *The Two Kargyupa Scriptures*. There is also a "treasure
text" (Tib. *gter nas bton*) source, but Tsongkhapa writes that he has no
confidence in it whatsoever. This is the only occasion in Lama

Tsongkhapa's writings in which he directly criticizes the [Nyingma/ Bon] treasure text tradition; I have not seen him do so elsewhere.

The two disciples who requested Tsongkhapa to write on the Six Yogas of Naropa were Miwang Drakpa Gyaltsen, who was the main sponsor of the Monlam Chenmo Festival, and his younger brother Sonam Gyaltsen.

In a concluding verse of *A Book of Three Inspirations* Tsongkhapa writes as follows concerning his purpose in composing his text,

> It contains clear instructions on the stages of meditation in
>   this path,
> A clear and critical guide to the principles in the trainings,
> And references to the authoritative tantras and commentaries
>   [on which the Six Yogas are based];
> These are the three features within which it is set.

These are probably the three "inspirations" referred to in the title.

Lama Jey Tsongkhapa's writings on the Six Yogas of Naropa are inconceivably profound guides to the practice of the Six Yogas of Naropa. Even if one searches throughout the three worlds of existence, one would find it difficult to discover a teaching equal to them.

We should exert ourselves in the study and practice of these teachings in order to take the essence of the opportunities and endowments afforded by our human life and thus accomplish enlightenment, that we may fulfill the aspirations of ourselves and others.

The colophon: Notes from a public reading of Jey Tsongkhapa's *A Book of Three Inspirations* given in the fourth month of the Fire Tiger Year at the request of Halha Zhab-drung.

4

Handprints of the Profound Path of the Six Yogas of Naropa: A Source of Every Realization

Tib. *Thabs lam na ro'i chos drug gi lag rjes dngos grub kun byung*

by

Gyalwa Wensapa Lobzang Dondrup
1505–1566

Translator's Preamble

Gyalwa Wensapa was one of the greatest Gelukpa yogis of the first half of the sixteenth century. Famous for his many years of meditation retreat in the Olkha Mountains, where Lama Tsongkhapa also spent five years in retreat, he is celebrated as one of the most eccentric of the Gelukpa monks to have achieved enlightenment in one lifetime. Unlike most Tibetan monks, who by tradition are humble and self-deprecating in expression, he was wild and arrogant, and used to say, "In the old days there was the great yogi Milarepa to represent the tradition of the mahasiddhas. Today there is just me."

He is also said to be one of the most important "pre-incarnations" of the lineage of Panchen Lamas. The First Panchen Lama (1568-1662), whose treatment of the Six Yogas is translated in Chapter Six, was his immediate reincarnation. Gyalwa Wensapa is not officially called one of the Panchens (because the title "Panchen Lama" was first given to Panchen Chokyi Gyaltsen by the Fifth Dalai Lama in the mid-1600s), but is always mentioned as a Panchen pre-incarnate.[1]

Gyalwa Wensapa's text on the Six Yogas does not deal with each of the six yogas individually, but instead looks at the underlying pillar on which the mansion of the Six Yogas is based, namely the tradition known in Tibetan as *sewa sum* (Tib. *sred-ba-gsum*), or "the three blendings."

There are many different ways to talk about these "three blendings." Tsongkhapa's *A Book of Three Inspirations* runs through several of these and dismisses many of them as meaningless distortions created by later Tibetan lamas. He then settles on what he considers to be the true doctrine as transmitted through Tilopa, Naropa, Marpa and Milarepa. As we will see in Chapter Five, his *A Practice Manual on the Six Yogas* also dedicates a section to the topic of the three blendings, the section being entitled "The Illusory Body and Clear Light Yogas."

Here he takes the three occasions for yogic practice—the waking state, the sleep/dream state, and the bardo state that follows death—and points out that the essence of the Six Yogas is to bring the three kayas—Dharmakaya, Sambhogakaya and Nirmanakaya—into each of the three states. Thus in fact there potentially are nine "blendings" to be accomplished, three for each of these three states.

In the Six Yogas tradition these three states—waking consciousness, sleep/dream consciousness, and after-death consciousness—are also known as the three bardos. Lama Tsongkhapa explains this in *A Book of Three Inspirations*,

> In this tradition [i.e., that of the Six Yogas of Naropa] we see three "bardo states" being mentioned. Firstly there is "the bardo between birth and death," which refers to the [waking-state] period from our birth to our death, including the present moment. Secondly there is "the dream bardo," which is the period between the moment of going to sleep and the moment of waking. Thirdly, the time from death until rebirth is known as "the bardo realm," or "the bardo of becoming."

The three blendings can be accomplished in any of these three bardos. As Tsongkhapa states in *A Book of Three Inspirations*, the most important of the three is the waking state bardo, for it is during the waking state that the average practitioner can most easily succeed in the tantric yogas, or at least lay the foundations of success. Once basic competency in the practice has been established in the waking state, one can apply the three blendings to the state of sleep and dreams. Finally, if one does not achieve full enlightenment during one's lifetime, either in the waking state or in the sleep/dream state, then one can apply the three blendings at the time of death and achieve enlightenment in the bardo.

Tsongkhapa writes in *A Book of Three Inspirations*,

> Those beings who do not possess yogic abilities will experience the three bardos as ordinary.... However, yogis holding the oral tradition teachings know how to take the three kayas at the time of the path [i.e., the ordinary dimensions of the three] and transform them into the three kayas at the time of the result [i.e., into buddhahood].

In Tibetan the tantric path is sometimes called *trebü-lam* (Tib. *'bres bu'i lam*), or "the resultant path," in order to convey the sense that for rapid enlightenment we can borrow an element of resultant enlightenment, bring it into the here-and-now of our unenlightened experience, and thus cause tremendous inner transformation. The idea is that we are never far away from enlightenment; we always have the ultimate and conventional realities at hand and the potentialities of the three kayas, but we just do not access them effectively.

Of the three kayas, the Dharmakaya is linked to our mind, Sambhogakaya to our speech, or communicative principle, and the Nirmanakaya to our ordinary body.

The process of the three blendings in brief is as follows.

We experience the clear light of the waking state naturally during sexual orgasm, and it can also be induced with yogic methods. Moreover, we naturally experience it at the moment of going to sleep, and at the moment of death. The principle here is that this clear light mind as experienced in each of the three occasions (waking, sleep and death) is the highest experience of our consciousness, and in it we dwell in a mental state of blissful, formless non-duality similar to that of the Dharmakaya wisdom of a buddha. Thus when we experience the clear light mind in any of these three occasions we should blend it with the Dharmakaya.

The first movement from this clear light mind is likened to the Sambhogakaya experience. In the waking state this occurs in our meditation when we fall out of the clear light that is induced with yogic techniques and the conceptual mind is aroused. In sleep it occurs after the clear light of the moment of entering sleep passes and we begin to dream. At death it occurs when the clear light flash at the moment of death passes and we leave our body and enter the bardo realm.

A buddha's Sambhogakaya is only visible to an arya, or saint, and not to an ordinary being; in the same way our thoughts, dreams, and bardo visions are not visible to ordinary beings but nonetheless are experiences of form. These subtle form experiences are to be linked to the natural realization of the illusory, blissful, and perfect nature of being; they are to be seen as an illusory theater made manifest for the benefit of the world. In other words, they are to be blended with the Sambhogakaya. This is the second set of three blendings.

The third blending is that of blending rebirth with the Nirmanakaya. Rebirth from the bardo of the waking state occurs every time that we arise from a meditation session and once more go about our ordinary life; rebirth from the bardo of the sleep/dream state occurs when we wake up and once more enter the work-a-day world; and rebirth from the bardo of becoming, or death bardo, occurs when we complete the unwinding process of the afterlife state and once again are ready to enter into a new body.

The basic principle underlying these three blendings is that what occurs to us at the time of death also occurs to us in miniature form at the time of going to sleep and can be induced in the waking state by means of the inner heat yogas.

For this reason it will be useful to explain how the yogic tradition speaks of the death experience. Tsongkhapa provides us with a brief description of this process in *A Practice Manual on the Six Yogas*,

> [At the time of death certain] external and internal signs of the energy dissolutions occur. First the earth element dissolves into the water element. The external sign is that one loses the ability to move one's limbs or control the body and has an appearance of total relaxation. There is a sensation as though one's body were sinking into the earth. The inner sign is a vision having a mirage-like quality. Next the water element dissolves into the fire element. The external sign is dryness of mouth and nose, and a shrivelling of the tongue. The inner sign is a vision as though of smoke. The fire element now dissolves into the air element. The external sign is that one's body heat begins to drop, withdrawing from the extremities [toward the heart]. The inner sign is a vision like that of seeing sparks, or of seeing a cluster of fireflies.
>
> Next the air element of conceptual thought dissolves into mind. Here the vital energies that support conceptual thought dissolve into consciousness. The external sign is that a long breath is exhaled, and the body seems unable to inhale. Even if one can inhale, one does so shallowly yet heavily. The inner sign is a vision of a light resembling that of a butterlamp undisturbed by wind movement.
>
> After this the first emptiness occurs, known simply as "emptiness." This is the experience of the vision known as "appearance." The inner sign is of whiteness, like seeing moonlight in a cloudless sky. The consciousness of "appearance" then dissolves into the second emptiness, known as "very empty." This is the experience of the vision known as "proximity." The inner vision is of a yellowish red light, like that of the light at sunrise. This dissolves into the third emptiness, "the great emptiness," which is linked to the experience of the vision known as "proximate attainment." The inner vision is of utter darkness, like that of a night sky pervaded by thick darkness. The person has a sensation of swooning and loses consciousness. After this the person emerges from the darkness and the state of mindlessness and arises into the experience of "utter emptiness," also termed "the clear light." The vision is of a color like the blending of the lights of sun and moon in a sky free from all darkness, like the clear sky at early dawn. This is the clear light that is the actual basis.

Sometimes we see it said that after the four elements have dissolved, the dissolutions of the conceptual mind are accompanied by the movement of the subtle drops of the body. First the white, male drop moves from the crown to the heart chakra, giving rise to an inner sign of a white light, called "the mind of appearance." Next the red, female drop moves up from the navel chakra to the heart, giving rise to a vision of a red light and "the mind of proximity." In the third phase the two drops collapse together at the heart, giving rise to a vision of an utterly dark light and "the mind of proximate attainment." Finally the two drops temporarily stabilize at the heart, giving rise to a vision of clear light and the experience called "the mind of clear light."

Ordinary people can stay in this clear light consciousness for a mere fraction of a second before their karmic instincts and psychological restlessness pull them away from it. The yogi learns to remain in it for a prolonged period of time, and to "blend the Dharmakaya" with it.

ENERGY DISSOLUTIONS AT THE TIME OF DEATH

Four Elemental Dissolutions

Dissolution	*Outer Sign*	*Inner Sign*
earth into water	body loses strength	like seeing a mirage
water into fire	dryness, shrivelling of tongue	like smoke
fire into air	body heat drops	like flickering fireflies
air into mind	long breath is exhaled	like the light of a butterlamp

Four "Emptiness" Dissolutions

Name	*Drop Movement*	*Inner Sign*
appearance/ first emptiness	white drop moves down	flash of white light
proximity/ second emptiness	red drop moves up	flash of red light
proximate attainment/ third emptiness	the two collapse together	utter darkness
clear light of death/ fourth emptiness	the two merge	clear light

We will see this sequence of four elemental dissolutions and four emptiness visions repeated several times in Gyalwa Wensapa's commentary to the Six Yogas, for the yogi or yogini trains to induce this death experience by means of his or her meditations and utilizes it in each of the stages of realizational experience generated in dependence on the Six Yogas.

In the Six Yogas system the elemental dissolutions are fabricated by means of withdrawing the subtle energies (called "airs" or "winds") away from their usual sites in the body and directing them into the central channel of the subtle vajra body, just as occurs at the time of death. As Gyalwa Wensapa puts it,

> The sign indicating that they have been caused to abide is that the visions of the elemental dissolutions and also the dissolution of the three visionary states occur. These dissolutions must be individually recognized.

Gyalwa Wensapa divides his treatise into two major sections: the techniques for drawing the energies into the central channel, and the techniques to be applied once this has been accomplished. In other words, the first stage of the Six Yogas is concerned with inducing this "death experience," and the second stage is concerned with what is to be accomplished from within the environment of the beyond-death state, when the bodily energies have been withdrawn and brought into the central channel.

The thrust of the dynamic of practicing in "the three bardos" is that in order to succeed in the yogic methods of working with the clear light of sleep and death (i.e., the clear light of the second two bardos), one must first succeed in the yogas of the waking state (i.e., the first of the three bardos). In *A Practice Manual on the Six Yogas* Tsongkhapa quotes Milarepa on this point,

> Jetsun Milarepa stated, "The clear light of death is Dharmakaya; one only must recognize it as such. In order to be able to do so, one should be introduced to it now by a supreme holy master. Cultivate an understanding of the essence of the view of the way things are, and train in the symbolic clear light of the path."

Also in *A Book of Three Inspirations* Tsongkhapa writes,

> The meditations on the three clear light consciousnesses—the clear light experienced through yogic endeavor in the waking state, the clear light of sleep, and the clear light of the moment of death— are similar in that success in all three applications depends upon first understanding the process of dissolving the vital energies and

consciousnesses into the central channel... and how thus to induce
the experience of the four emptinesses and four blisses.

Because the ability to dissolve the subtle energies into the central channel and thus induce the state of the clear light consciousness is accomplished by means of the inner heat yoga, the inner heat practice is
called "the foundation stone of the path of the Six Yogas."

The Dharmakaya is a buddha's formless nature, and with us it is
linked to the clear light consciousness, in which there is no sense of
duality or multiplicity. In *The Guhyasamaja Tantra* a parallel is drawn
with our experience at the moment of sexual orgasm, wherein we experience only bliss, radiance and a sense of oneness with the world.
These three mental qualities are briefly present at the time of ordinary
sexual orgasm, and also are induced with yogic methods in the orgasmic bliss produced by the inner heat yoga. This state of mind provides the perfect environment for bringing a buddha's Dharmakaya
reality into the continuum of our own experience.

Sometimes the term "inner heat karmamudra" is used, because
many practitioners rely upon a karmamudra, or sexual partner, in order to induce the desired experience. Here the inner heat yoga is called
"the inner condition" and the karmamudra sexual practice is called
"the outer condition." The two are practiced in conjunction with one
another in order to harness the natural energy process of the sexual
experience to the yogic methods for energy control.

In other words, the parallel between sexual orgasm and the bliss
required to succeed in the inner heat yoga means that the advanced
stages of the inner heat yoga are often best practiced while in sexual
union. This is done in order to induce the "four blisses" or "four joys"
that we see mentioned in most texts on the Six Yogas. The idea is that
after the energies are brought into the central channel one draws the
drops through the four (or five) chakras; as they move from chakra to
chakra they give rise to an according experience of bliss. This bliss is
like that of sexual orgasm, with the exception that it is sustained for
long periods of time. The most important of these four blisses is the
fourth, which is known as "the innate bliss." It is this bliss that is most
closely akin to the Dharmakaya experience, and in which "the blending with Dharmakaya" is to be accomplished. In the Six Yogas system
this is also known as "meditating on the innate wisdom."

Gyalwa Wensapa recommends that we take up the karmamudra
practice at five specific stages in the training of the Six Yogas.
Tsongkhapa describes the technique of controlling the sexual drops in

A Practice Manual on the Six Yogas, although he does not distinguish between when this is accomplished by means of solo practice and when with a sexual partner, because in any case the principle is the same.

Here in the waking state one applies the inner heat yoga in order to draw the energies into the central channel and give rise to an experience of clear light resembling that at the moments of sleep and death. The clear light consciousness that is aroused by means of the yoga is to be retained and "blended with the Dharmakaya." This is the waking state practice.

When going to sleep one observes the natural process of the elemental dissolutions and enhances the experience by means of yogic application. The preparation is the waking-state practice of becoming familiar with the energy transformations that lead up to the experience. As soon as the elemental energies have withdrawn and the four emptiness experiences begin naturally to occur, one watches for the arisal of the clear light consciousness of sleep and blends it with the Dharmakaya.

Similarly, at death one allows the energy withdrawals to occur naturally, and when the clear light arises one applies the techniques of retaining it. One then blends the Dharmakaya with it. Working in this way with these three—i.e., blending with the clear lights of the waking state (induced by yogic methods), sleep state, and death state—is known as "blending Dharmakaya with the clear light of the three occasions."

Again, all three of the Dharmakaya blendings depend on having first achieved success in the waking-state practice of the inner heat yoga.

Beginners in the practice will only be able to bathe in the clear light Dharmakaya for a few moments. Then the instincts carried by the ordinary mind will begin to make themselves felt, and they will drift into thoughts. This is when the "waking state bardo" is to be "blended with the Sambhogakaya." Similarly, novice practitioners will not be able to stabilize the clear light of sleep for long; karmic instincts, memories, habits, bodily energies, and so forth will begin to make themselves felt, and they will drift off into dreams. Here the "bardo of dreams" is to be blended with the Sambhogakaya. In the same way, in the death experience the clear light of death soon gives way to form aspects, such as memories and karmic predispositions, and one falls from the clear light of death into a hallucinated bardo, or after-death experience; this after-death bardo is to be blended with the Sambhogakaya at that time.

Here the term "Sambhogakaya" refers to the higher of a buddha's two form aspects, the other being the Nirmanakaya, or coarse form.

The third blending involves bringing the "rebirthing" experience of the three occasions into the Nirmanakaya perspective. For example, in the waking state, at the completion of our yogic session we arise from meditation and return to the ordinary world; this experience is to be blended with the illusory emanation body, or manner in which a buddha sends countless emanations out into the world in order to benefit others. After sleep and dreams we wake up and go about our everyday life; again, this is to be blended with the idea of Nirmanakaya and conscious emanation. Third, after death and the bardo we may have to take rebirth; this is to be done as a conscious yogic application of emanation.

All six yogas of the Naropa system are based on the principles of these three blendings. These three are what transform the yogas from mere calisthenics into enlightenment techniques.

The section of Tsongkhapa's *A Practice Manual on the Six Yogas* introducing the illusory body and clear light doctrines explains the process of the three blendings with wonderful lucidity (see pages 118-123 below). As he explained in *A Book of Three Inspirations*, Tsongkhapa felt that the Tibetans had tampered with this doctrine of the three blendings and brought to it various meanings that have nothing to do with the original teachings of Tilopa, Naropa, Marpa and Milarepa. For example, he felt that the popularly taught doctrine of blending the three delusions—lust, aversion and confusion—with the three kayas lacks any sense whatsoever. Although these three *kleshas* are incorporated into the tantric path of the Six Yogas of Naropa, he does not agree that the popular presentation of the technique is relevant to the discussion of the three blendings; on the contrary, to bring them in not only is superficial and arbitrary, but also mistakes the gist of the process.[2]

Another noteworthy feature of Gyalwa Wensapa's text is that he links the process of the attainment of enlightenment to the levels of realization as expressed in the tantric terminology of the *Guhyasamaja Tantra*. That is to say, the tantric yogas transport the practitioner through the successive stages of body isolation, speech isolation, unpurified illusory body, semblant clear light, ultimate clear light, and then purified illusory body. The process culminates in the attainment of "the great union still in training," and finally "the great union beyond training," which is complete enlightenment. He then reverses his discussion and goes step-by-step from the highest stage of realization, or the full enlightenment that is beyond training, back to the basic levels of practice, to illustrate how enlightenment as taught in the tantras is a graduated path, and that one proceeds successively from initial beginnings to the highest attainment.

His treatment of "the three blendings" is brilliant, and I have not found anything in Tibetan literature to compare with it for sheer simplicity and profundity.

Handprints of the Profound Path of the Six Yogas of Naropa: A Source of Every Realization

by Gyalwa Wensapa Lobzang Dondrup

Homage to Guru Vajradhara, together with the myriad of mandala deities.[3]

To engage in the practice of Naropa's Six Yogas one must understand three subjects: the reality of the basis; the stages of traversing the path; and the manner of manifesting the results.

THE REALITY OF THE BASIS

The reality of the basis of our experience involves three subjects: the reality of the body; that of the mind; and that shared by both the body and mind.

The Reality of the Body

The reality of the body is that it is threefold: coarse, subtle, and very subtle.

The coarse body is the ordinary body made of flesh, blood and bone, and born from the sperm and ovum of our parents.

The subtle body refers to the abiding energy channels, the flowing energies, and the emplaced red and white [i.e., female and male] creative drops.

The very subtle body is the subtle energy that supports the consciousness of the four emptinesses, especially the fourth emptiness, called "utter emptiness," which is the clear light mind.

The Reality of the Mind

As for the mind, it also has these three same dimensions: coarse, subtle, and very subtle.

The coarse mind refers to that co-emergent with the five sensory consciousnesses.

The subtle mind is that co-emergent with the driving force of the six root distortions, the twenty secondary distortions, and the eighty conceptual mindsets.

The very subtle mind is the dimension of consciousness that is in the same nature as the four emptinesses, and especially the fourth, "utter emptiness," which is the clear light mind.

The Reality Shared by the Body and Mind

When embodied sentient beings meet with death, the very subtle aspects of their vital energies and consciousness become of one entity. This entity is the reality shared by both body and mind.

THE STAGES OF TRAVERSING THE PATH

The stages of traversing the path involve two principal types of techniques: those for drawing the vital energies into the central channel, and those that are applied after the energies have been drawn in [to the central channel].

The Techniques for Drawing the Vital Energies into the Central Channel

The technique for drawing the vital energies into the central channel begins with generating the image of oneself as Buddha Vajradhara, male and female in sexual union, and envisioning the energy channels together with the mantric syllables at the chakras. One then meditates on the inner heat and on the melting drops. This causes the vital energies to enter, abide, and dissolve.

The sign indicating the entering of the vital energies is that, when a breath is inhaled in order to test one's progress, the air flows evenly through both nostrils. The sign indicating that the energies have been caused to abide is that the visions of the elemental dissolutions and also the dissolution of the three visionary states occur. These dissolutions must be individually recognized.

First earth dissolves into water, and there is a vision like seeing a mirage. Then water dissolves into fire, and there is a smoke-like vision. Next fire dissolves into air, and there is a vision like flickering fireflies. The air element begins to dissolve into the visionary consciousness called "appearance," and there is a vision like that of the glow of a butterlamp. Air fully dissolves into "appearance," and there is a vision of whiteness, like a clear autumn sky pervaded by the light of the full moon. This dissolves into the consciousness known as "proximity," and there is a vision of redness, like that of the clear sky pervaded by sunlight. This dissolves into "proximate attainment," and there is a vision of overwhelming darkness, like the sky before dawn, with neither sun nor moon. "Proximate attainment" then dissolves into the clear light; there is a vision of clear radiance, like the sky at daybreak, free from the three conditions. One must recognize these experiences as they occur. This is the process known as "blending with Dharmakaya during the waking state."

When the time comes to arise from the clear light absorption one arouses the strong instinct to put aside one's old aggregates and arise in the form of a Buddha Vajradhara, male and female in union. Then when one arises from the clear light one's old aggregates will be set aside and within the mind there forms the image of a Buddha Vajradhara, male and female in union. Simultaneously one applies the techniques for inducing the stages of dissolution [described above] in reverse order. Thus one goes from the clear light to proximate attainment, to proximity, and to appearance. One experiences the signs of the elemental dissolutions [in reverse]: a glow like that of a butterlamp, firefly-like sparks, smoke, and finally the mirage. This is the process known as "blending with the Sambhogakaya during the waking state."

One engages in the stages of meditation on transformations associated with that Sambhogakaya form and focuses one's absorption upon it. When one decides to arise from the absorption, one does so by meditating upon one's old aggregates as the Symbolic Being (Skt. *samayasattva*), with the Wisdom Being (Skt. *jnanasattva*) at the heart. This is the process known as "blending with Nirmanakaya during the waking state."

Simultaneous with this, as the air begins to flow through the nostrils again and the five sensory consciousnesses are revived, whatever appearances occur are seen as emptiness, emptiness as bliss, and bliss as the mandala and its deities. This is the practice to be cultivated in the post-meditation sessions.

Similarly, when one goes to sleep one attempts to retain the clear light of sleep and sets the resolution to arise as a Sambhogakaya deity in the dream state. As one prepares for sleep one engages in the meditations on the channels, energies, and chakras, causing the drops to melt and the blisses to arise. The vital energies enter, abide, and dissolve within the central channel. All the signs of the dissolution process occur, from "earth into water," until the emergence of the clear light. The four emptinesses emerge in the nature of the four blisses. At the same time as the clear light occurs, one engages in meditation on bliss conjoined with [the wisdom of] emptiness. This is the process known as "blending with Dharmakaya in sleep."

When the time comes to arise from that clear light one generates the resolution to arise with a dream body by setting aside the body of the old aggregates and taking the form of a Buddha Vajradhara, male and female in union. Then when one emerges from the clear light [of sleep] the dream body appears. However, one does not do so in the body of the old aggregates; instead, one's dream body arises to the mind as a Buddha Vajradhara, male and female in union. This is what is known as "blending with Sambhogakaya in dreams."

One focuses one's absorption on the meditations of the transformative processes of that Sambhogakaya. When the time comes to awaken from sleep, one does so by emerging with one's old aggregates envisioned as the Symbolic Being and with the Wisdom Being at one's heart. This is the process known as "blending with Nirmanakaya while awakening."

Simultaneous with this, as the air begins to flow through the nostrils and the five sensory consciousnesses revive, whatever appearances occur are seen as emptiness, emptiness as bliss, and bliss as the mandala deities. This is the practice to be cultivated in the post-meditation sessions.

The yogi who is not able to accomplish the realizations of the highest stage before the time of death should cultivate the resolution to apply the techniques for retaining the clear light of death, arising in the Sambhogakaya in the bardo, and taking birth with the incarnation of a tantric master, or *mantracharyin*. Then as the actual moment of death draws near one should meditate on the channels, energies, chakras and so forth as above, and meditate upon the blazing and melting. This causes the vital energies to enter into the central channel and to abide and dissolve, giving rise to the signs of the dissolutions, until the signs of the clear light occur. As the clear light of death emerges one focuses in meditation upon emptiness. This is the process known as "blending with Dharmakaya at death."

When the time comes to arise from the clear light one arouses the instinct to set aside the old aggregates and, in taking a bardo body, to arise in the form of a Buddha Vajradhara, male and female in union. Then as one emerges from the clear light the image of the bardo body arises as Buddha Vajradhara, male and female in union, and the old aggregates are set aside. Simultaneously the signs of the dissolution process manifest in reverse, as consciousness reverses through the stages of clear light to proximate attainment, and so forth, until the vision of the mirage. This is the process known as "blending with Sambhogakaya in the bardo."

One remains focused on the stages of absorption in the meditations of the Sambhogakaya transformations. Then when the wish to take rebirth forms, one seeks a suitable genetic environment in the white and red drops [i.e., the fertilized seeds] of one's future parents, in order to achieve rebirth as the special body-vessel of a tantric master. This is the process known as "blending with Nirmanakaya at rebirth."

The sentient being who enters the womb in this way will go through the five stages of growth in the womb, such as that of being just a small conglomerate of cells, and so forth. That being will then leave the womb, go through childhood and youth, and then enter into spiritual practice and complete the remainder of the path, thus achieving Buddhahood.

The Technique to be Applied After the Energies Have Been Drawn In [to the Central Channel]

After applying oneself to these methods for directing the vital energies into the central channel, one eventually achieves a mature meditative absorption fluent in the process. Soon one perceives the signs of approaching the stage wherein the illusory body can be produced. From within the sphere of sexually uniting with a karmamudra, which is the outer supporting condition, one engages the inner supporting condition, which refers to meditation on the channels, chakras, and so forth, and meditation upon the blazing and melting. The vital energies are caused to enter into the central channel and to abide and dissolve, giving rise to the signs of the dissolutions, from the mirage and so forth until the sign of the clear light. The four emptinesses emerge in the nature of the four blisses. When the innate clear light arises, one meditates upon bliss conjoined with emptiness. This is the technique for engaging the innate semblant clear light, with which the basis of the illusory body is produced.

When the time comes to emerge from the clear light, one arouses the instinct to set aside one's old aggregates and to take the form of a Buddha Vajradhara, male and female in union. Then as one arises from the clear light, the vital energy of the five radiances, upon which rides the innate semblant clear light, serves as the substantial cause; and the mind serves as the simultaneously present condition. Based upon these, the old aggregates are by-passed and one arises in the form of a Buddha Vajradhara, male and female in union, adorned by the marks and signs of perfection. This is the stage of "the unpurified illusory body." Simultaneously one experiences the dissolution process in reverse, going from clear light to proximate attainment, and so forth, until the sign of the mirage.

In tantric systems such as Guhyasamaja this illusory body is illustrated and explained by using twelve similes.[4]

At that time three factors occur simultaneously: the cessation of the innate semblance [i.e., the "semblant" or "metaphoric" clear light consciousness], the fulfillment of proximate attainment in the dissolution process, and arisal in the actual form of an "unpurified illusory body." The person with that illusory body then focuses on the stages of absorption.

How does one engage the stages of absorption?

First one meditates on the phases of the dissolution process, which causes the vital energies to enter into the central channel, abide, and dissolve. This gives rise to the signs of the absorptions, from the mirage up to the clear light. When the time comes to emerge from the clear light, one arouses the resolution to have the unpurified illusory body transform into a pure illusory body. Then as one arises from the clear light the unpurified illusory body is set aside and the image of the pure illusory body arises within the mind. Simultaneous with that, one experiences the dissolution process in reverse; one moves from the clear light to proximate attainment, and so forth, until the sign of the mirage. The being engaging that Sambhogakaya form then arises as the Nirmanakaya, emanating forth the supported and supporting mandalas. When one wants to arise from meditation one does so by meditating upon the old aggregates as the Symbolic Being with the Wisdom Being at the heart.

Residing within that vessel one shows the Dharma to trainees and cultivates the activities of the after-practice, which include tantric enactments such as eating, drinking, and sexually uniting with a karmamudra.

The practitioner of this illusory body stage cultivates these advanced meditations and eventually sees signs that the accomplishment of the stage known as "the great union of training" is approaching. He engages in the practice of uniting with a karmamudra as the external condition; and, as the inner condition, engages the meditations on the stages of the dissolutions and so forth, causing the vital energies to enter the central channel, abide, and dissolve. The signs of the dissolutions occur, from that of the mirage to that of the clear light. The four emptinesses emerge in the nature of the four blisses. At the moment of the innate clear light, one engages the meditation of bliss conjoined with emptiness.

At that time five factors occur simultaneously: the state known as "proximate attainment in the unfoldment process" ceases; the innate bliss induces an unprecedented direct realization of emptiness; the illusory body is purified in the actual clear light, appearing like a rainbow in a radiant sky; one achieves the unhindered stage wherein the direct antidote to the emotional obscurations is born within one's mindstream; and one's continuum becomes that of an arya.

By the time the process of emerging from the clear light begins, one's previous driving force in the practice will have come into play, placing one at the door through which the "pure illusory body" can be achieved. As one emerges from the clear light, with the role of the substantial cause being played by the subtle energy of five radiances, upon which rides the innate actuality [i.e., the innate actual clear light consciousness], and the role of the simultaneously present condition being played by the mind itself, one arises in the actual "pure illusory body," which flows in an unbroken stream in a form such as that of Buddha Vajradhara, male and female in union, adorned by the marks and signs of perfection, with one's old aggregates left behind.

Simultaneously the signs of the dissolution process in reverse manifest, from that of going from the clear light to proximate attainment, until the sign of the mirage. At that time five factors occur together: the innate actuality ceases; the state of proximate attainment in the dissolution process is produced; the arisal of the "pure illusory body"; one achieves the path of utter liberation which is free from emotional obscurations;[5] and one's continuum becomes that of an arhat.

The being of that Sambhogakaya form then focuses in meditative absorption.

What are the stages of that absorption? One focuses in single-pointed meditation upon emptiness and then causes the vital energies to enter into the central channel, to abide, and to dissolve, giving rise to the signs, until the clear light occurs. At that time one has arrived at the place wherein the state of great union can be unobstructedly achieved, where body and mind can be brought together as a single entity. Here body is represented by the pure illusory body adorned with the marks and signs of perfection, and mind is represented by the actual clear light consciousness.

When the time comes to arise from that clear light experience one's previous driving force from the practice comes into play, and one finds oneself at the door through which the body of "the great union in training" can become that of "the great union beyond training." In emerging from the clear light, the being on the stage of "the great union of training" perceives the image of the body of the stage of "the great union beyond training." Simultaneously the signs of the reversal process occur, from that of moving from the clear light to proximate attainment, and so forth, until the mirage.

That Sambhogakaya holds the potential of the Nirmanakaya, which emanates forth a net of activities, such as manifesting the supported and supporting mandalas.

When one wishes to arise from meditation, one enters into one's own old aggregates or some other old aggregates, whichever is appropriate. Then, residing in that vessel, one shows Dharma to those to be trained and cultivates the after-practice activities, such as uniting with a karmamudra, eating and drinking, as well as residing with wild animals, and so forth.

THE MANNER OF MANIFESTING THE RESULTS

The yogi on the stage of great union of training cultivates the absorptions of that level during both formal meditation and post-meditation sessions, and eventually sees signs of the approach of the attainment of great union beyond training. One engages the external condition of sexually uniting with a karmamudra and the internal condition of meditating single-pointedly on emptiness, causing the vital energies to enter into the central channel, abide, and dissolve. The signs occur, beginning with the mirage and so forth, until eventually the signs of the clear light manifest. The four emptinesses arise in the nature of the four blisses.

The moment this innate clear light manifests, one engages the meditation of bliss conjoined with [the wisdom of] emptiness. The first moment of this clear light is the unobstructed stage on which the perceptual obscurations[6] are transcended. The second moment of it is also the first moment of omniscient buddhahood, wherein one remains in perfect absorption upon the final nature of being, while at the same time directly seeing all conventional realities as clearly as a piece of fruit held in the hand. The body of great union of training becomes the great union beyond training, the actual Sambhogakaya endowed with the kisses of the seven excellences that sends out thousands of Nirmanakaya emanations to benefit those to be trained. Thus one achieves complete buddhahood in the nature of the three kayas.

As a preliminary to attaining the stage of the great union beyond training, one must go through the stage of great union of training. As a preliminary to that one must accomplish the illusory body, and for that one must first meditate upon the channels, chakras, blazing, melting, and so forth.

In turn, as a preliminary [to these completion stage practices] one must go to the end of the coarse and subtle generation stage practices which take birth, death, and bardo, the bases to be purified, as the paths of the three kayas. For this one must have received the complete empowerments and be mature in observing the disciplines adopted at the time of initiation. Moreover, before entering into tantric practice one should train the mind in the common path, from cultivating an effective working relationship with a spiritual master, up to the meditative training that combines shamata and vipassyana.

Thus the jewel-like practitioner who engages in the profound path of Naropa's Six Yogas in this way has entered into a complete and unmistaken path for accomplishing enlightenment in one short lifetime, even in this degenerate age.

The colophon: Notes on the stream of teachings of Vajradhara Lobzang Dondrup, with nothing extra and nothing left out, transcribed and edited by the Buddhist monk Basowa Tenpai Gyaltsen.[7]

5

A Practice Manual on the Six Yogas of Naropa: Taking the Practice in Hand

Tib. *Na ro'i chos drug gi dmigs skor lag tu len tshul*

by

Lama Jey Tsongkhapa
1357–1419

Translator's Preamble

The collected works of Lama Jey Tsongkhapa, the founder of the Geluk school, contain two texts on the Six Yogas of Naropa: a *tri-yig* (Tib. *'khrid yig*), or treatise of the tradition; and a *mig-rim* (Tib. *dmigs rim*), or "Stages of Meditation/Visualization."

The *tri-yig*, included in *Tsongkhapa's Six Yogas of Naropa*, is double the length of the latter, and is written as a critical study of the overall nature of the system, including philosophical and historical points of controversy and interest.

A *mig-rim*, on the other hand, is usually written in the form of quintessential meditation instruction combined with liturgy. This is the case with Tsongkhapa's *mig-rim* on the Six Yogas. It directly presents the practice of the system of the Six Yogas, and when reading the text one has to keep this in mind. Its strength lies in the fact that it provides a succinct overview of the meditations and yogas of the tradition. The instructions on the Six Yogas given here in brief by Tilopa and Naropa respectively in Chapters One and Two, touched upon by Jey Sherab Gyatso in Chapter Three and presented from the viewpoint of the three blendings by Gyalwa Wensapa in Chapter Four, are detailed here by Tsongkhapa as step-by-step methods in practice.

Lama Jey Tsongkhapa was born in 1357 in Amdo near Tibet's border with China to a family of farmers. His birth was accompanied by many auspicious signs, and as a child he became a monk. By the time he reached his teens he had become learned in the sutras and tantras and proficient in meditation. His teacher sent him to Central Tibet to complete his training, and over the years to follow he studied in forty-five monasteries and hermitages under all the greatest lamas of his day.

When he had finally become content with the level of his learning, he entered into the traditional four-year retreat and dedicated himself to intense meditation. Shortly thereafter he entered another retreat, and a year into the process achieved realization.

The later years of his life were dedicated to teaching, writing, and the creation of spiritual centers. The most important of his building activities was the construction of Ganden Monastery in 1409, which soon became the fountainhead of the spiritual movement that followed in his wake. In the early days this school of Tibetan Buddhism was known as the Galuk, or "Joyful Tradition" (from the name of his monastery, Ganden, or "Place of Joy"). In later times the sect changed its name to Geluk, or "Sublime Tradition."

Thousands of disciples came to him for training, of whom five are said to have been supreme. From among these, the youngest was a monk who later became known to history as the First Dalai Lama. All subsequent Dalai Lamas, including the present (or Fourteenth), have received their basic monastic training from lamas of the Geluk school founded by Lama Tsongkhapa.

Tsongkhapa's approach to Buddhist study and practice was one of balance. The era in which he lived was intensely spiritual in character, but was afflicted by a polarization of the Buddhist communities into semi-literate yogis dwelling in mountain caves and monks who were highly learned but weak in the practice of meditation. Tsongkhapa insisted that all the disciples who came to him become well-versed in the Buddhist classics, and also that they practice daily meditation and undertake the major retreats. In addition, the Tibetan population was polarized into those who devoted themselves to the sutra (or General Mahayana) aspect of Dharma, and those who dedicated themselves to the tantric path; Tsongkhapa insisted that all his disciples first gain basic inner stability by means of the General Mahayana trainings and then enter into the exalted tantric yogas.

His formula certainly met with success, and Gelukpa monasteries and hermitages grew up throughout Central Asia at an amazing rate. Within a matter of a few centuries the Geluk had outgrown all other sects of Tibetan Buddhism combined. This was not only the case within Tibet, but also within much of Central Asia. For example, even during his lifetime seventeen Gelukpa monasteries and temples were established in China by one of his disciples. Moreover, the Geluk tradition of Tibetan Buddhism became the national religion of the Mongol nations in 1578, when the Third Dalai Lama travelled and taught there at the invitation of the Chakkar king Altan Khan, and it has remained so ever since.

Tsongkhapa was an amazingly prolific writer. His texts on the principal subjects of the Sutrayana, such as Madhyamaka and Prajnaparamita, stand today with the great classics of Asian literature. However, his writings on the tantric path are even more important, and certainly more voluminous.

His treatise on the Six Yogas of Naropa, *A Book of Three Inspirations*, is one of his most popular tantric writings, and is often used as the basis of public discourses given by Gelukpa lamas on the Six Yogas. His *Practice Manual on the Six Yogas of Naropa* is less well-known, because it is usually only taught to practitioners in retreat. It nonetheless is regarded as an important tantric work.

Even though his *Practice Manual on the Six Yogas* is always published as part of Tsongkhapa's Collected Works, in fact it was not actually written by him. Instead, it was compiled from a number of his teachings and then edited as a cohesive text by Sempa Chenpo Kunzangpa, one of his immediate disciples and also a guru to the First Dalai Lama. However, in that it was compiled from Tsongkhapa's words it is always attributed directly to him.

The text opens with liturgies for the meditations on Vajrasattva and guru yoga, followed by a brief sadhana of Heruka Chakrasamvara. These are all regarded as preliminary practices which anyone wishing to engage in the Six Yogas should complete. Most trainees would be expected to perform 100,000 recitations of the Vajrasattva hundred-syllable mantra, together with the according meditations, and also 100,000 recitations of the guru's mantra in conjunction with the meditations described in the liturgy. These two methods are usually done in retreat, and generally take a month to six weeks each to complete. In addition trainees would perform at least a three-month retreat on their mandala deity, with many hundreds of thousands of mantra recitations. As Jey Sherab Gyatso states, the most common mandala deity used in conjunction with the Six Yogas is Heruka Chakrasamvara.

A Practice Manual on the Six Yogas of Naropa: Taking the Practice in Hand

by Lama Jey Tsongkhapa

Homage to the lotus feet of the spiritual master, who is inseparable in nature from Buddha Vajradhara.

The instructions on the practice of the profound path renowned everywhere as the Six Yogas of Naropa are presented under two headings: (I) the special tantric preliminaries; and (II) on the basis of having completed the preliminaries, how to meditate on the actual tantric path.

THE SPECIAL TANTRIC PRELIMINARIES

There are two special tantric preliminary practices to be completed before one can take up the meditations on the Six Yogas of Naropa: the meditation and mantra recitation of Vajrasattva; and the meditation on guru yoga.

THE VAJRASATTVA MEDITATION AND MANTRA RECITATION

Begin by blending thoughts of refuge and the universalist bodhisattva attitude deeply into your mindstream. Then meditate as follows:

Above your head visualize a white syllable *PAM*. It transforms into a white lotus with a white syllable *AH* resting upon it. This syllable transforms into a moon disk with a white syllable *HUM* resting above it. *HUM* transforms into a white, five-pronged vajra marked by a syllable *HUM*.

Lights go out from this, accomplish the two purposes, and then absorb into it again.

This transforms, and Vajrasattva instantly appears [upon the lotus and moon seats on your head]. His body is white in color, he holds a vajra in his right hand and a bell in his left, and is embracing the consort white Vajra Bhagavati. She holds a curved knife and a cup made of a human skull. They are adorned with the precious ornaments and have the marks and signs of perfection. Vajrasattva is seated with his legs crossed in the vajra posture.

A white syllable *HUM* stands upon a moon disk at his heart. From it lights emanate forth and summon the Wisdom Beings, who resemble him.

Make the five types of devotional offerings to them. Then: *JAH HUM BAM HOH!* They are summoned, and dissolve into, merge with, and become inseparably one with him.

Again lights emanate from the syllable *HUM* at Vajrasattva's heart, summoning the Initiation Deities.

One again makes the devotional offerings to them and then recites: "O Tathagatas, You Gone to Suchness, please bestow empowerment."

The Tathagatas agree to bestow empowerment. Their consorts hold up jewelled vases filled with wisdom empowerment nectars, and sing the auspicious verse,

> Just as at the time of the Buddha's birth
> Celestial beings appeared and bathed him,
> So do we bathe you now
> With these mystical empowerment nectars.
> *OM SARVA TATHAGATA ABHISHEKATA SAMAYA
>   SHRI YA HUM.*

Saying this, they pour forth empowering nectars from their vases, until the body of Vajrasattva and Consort are completely filled with the wisdom nectars. Buddha Akshobya manifests from the overflow as Vajrasattva's crown ornament.

One calls out, "O Bhagavan Vajrasattva, please inspire me to purify all negative karmic seeds, spiritual obscurations, and degenerated precepts accumulated by myself and others."

Requested in this way, lights emanate forth from the syllable *HUM* at his heart. They touch all living beings and purify them of negative karmic instincts, obscurations, and transgressions of spiritual precepts.

The lights then present devotional offerings to the buddhas and bodhisattvas of the ten directions. The blessings of body, speech, mind, realization, and activity power of all enlightened beings transform into light and are drawn into the syllable *HUM* at Vajrasattva's heart. Vajrasattva becomes brilliantly radiant and empowered with every strength and perfection.

Surrounding the syllable *HUM* at Vajrasattva's heart are the syllables of the hundred-syllable mantra: *OM VAJRA HERUKA SAMAYA / MANUPALAYA / HERUKA TVENOPATISHTHA / DRIDHO MEBHAVA / SUTOSHYO MEBHAVA / SUPOSHYO MEBHAVA / ANURAKTO MEBHAVA / SARVA SIDDHI MEPRAYACHHA / SARVA KARMA SUCHAME / CHHITAM SHRI YAM / KURU HUM/ HA HA HA HA HOH BHAGAVAN / VAJRA HERUKA MAME MUCHA / HERUKA BHAVA / MAHA SAMAYA SATTVA AH.*

Lights emanate from these mantric syllables. They purify living beings of negative karmic instincts and spiritual obscurations, and make inconceivably vast offerings to the buddhas and bodhisattvas. The inspiring energies of the body, speech, and mind of the buddhas and bodhisattvas are drawn forth and are absorbed into the mantric syllables.

A stream of white nectar flows forth from the mantric seeds. It flows down inside the bodies of Vajrasattva and Consort, exiting them from the place of their sexual union. The nectars enter my body via the crown aperture, until my body is utterly filled. All negative karmic instincts and obscurations collected by means of activities of body, speech, and mind are expelled and leave via my bodily apertures and pores in the form of a thick black mist. I become purified of all negative karma and obscurations. The stream of wisdom nectar fills my body with a blazing white radiance, infusing me with every spiritual knowledge and excellence.

Meditating in this way, recite the hundred-syllable mantra as many times as possible. Then recite:

> I, confused by unknowing, have
> Occasionally failed in keeping the precepts.
> O guru protector, inspire me.
> Especially, O Buddha Vajrasattva,
> Whose nature is great compassion,
> King of living beings, grant refuge.

Vajrasattva replies, "Child of good character, your negative karmic instincts, spiritual obscurations and failures in training are all now purified."

He then dissolves into me. My body, speech, and mind become inseparably one with the body, speech, and mind of Vajrasattva.

THE MEDITATION ON GURU YOGA

Meditate as follows:

In the space in front of you, on a jeweled throne supported by eight lions, is a seat made of a lotus with a sun disk. Upon this sits your guru in the form of Buddha Vajradhara. His body is blue in color, and he has one face and two arms. He holds a vajra in his right hand and a bell in his left, and embraces a consort who resembles him. His upper and lower robes are made of celestial silks, and he is adorned with the jewel ornaments. His legs are crossed in the vajra posture, and he is ablaze with lights of five colors.

A white syllable *OM* rests upon a moon disk at his crown chakra; a red syllable *AH* rests upon a lotus at his throat chakra; and a blue syllable *HUM* rests upon a sun disk at his heart chakra. All three syllables are ablaze with lights.

Lights emanate from the syllable *HUM*, summoning forth Buddha Vajradhara, the assembly of lineage gurus, and the host of mandala meditational deities. They all dissolve into the Buddha Vajradhara visualized in front.

Now make devotional offerings, and then offer the mandala symbolic of the universe:

> *OM VAJRA BHUMI AH HUM!* Here is the great powerful golden earth. *OM VAJRA REKHE AH HUM!* Here is the surrounding iron fence. Here is the great Mount Meru; to the east of it, the continent Lupakpo; to the south, Jambuling; to the west Balangcho; and to the north Draminyan. Here also are the sub-continents: Lu and Lupak; Ngayab and Ngayabzhan; Yodan and Lamchokdro; Draminyan and Draminyan Kyida.
>
> Here are the precious elephant, the precious lord, the precious supreme horse, the precious queen, the precious warrior, the precious wheel, the precious jewel, and the precious treasure vase. And here are the sun and the moon.
>
> In this way I create a symbolic universe with all auspicious things in it, visualizing it as being made of various precious gems. I send it forth, gems together with the mass of meritorious energy collected in the past, present, and future by myself and all other living beings through our actions of body, speech, and mind, and

together with our pleasures of the three times, as an offering in
the manner exemplified by the great bodhisattva Samantabhadra.
All of this I envision within my mind and offer to my gurus,
meditational deities, and the forces of spiritual refuge. Accept it
out of your compassion, and bestow waves of inspiring power
upon me.

In this way offer the mandala to the guru inseparable from Buddha
Vajradhara. This should be done as outer, inner, and secret offerings.
Here the flower petals, or whatever substances are used, represent the
outer offering. The nectars with which these are anointed represent
the inner offering.

Then recite the following verse and request:

> Through the guru's kindness the state of great bliss
> In a single moment can be accomplished.
> O precious guru, who is like a wish-fulfilling jewel,
> I pay homage at your lotus feet.

"O precious master, bestow blessings that I may be inspired to quickly
generate within my mindstream the realizations of the ordinary and
extraordinary paths. Bestow blessings that any negative conditions
obstructing the fulfillment of my aspirations may be pacified, and that
conducive conditions may prevail."

The guru smiles with delight. White lights emanate forth from the
white syllable *OM* at his crown, and enter your body via your crown.
They fill you with a white radiance, purify all negative karma collected by means of the body, bestow the vase empowerment, and plant
seeds for the attainment of the vajra body.

Red lights then emanate forth from the red syllable *AH* at his throat
and enter your body via your throat. They fill you with a red radiance, purify all negative karma collected by means of speech, bestow
the secret empowerment, and plant seeds for the attainment of the
vajra speech.

Blue lights emanate forth from the blue syllable *HUM* at his heart
and enter your body via your heart. They fill you with a blue radiance, purify all negative karma collected by means of the mind, bestow the wisdom awareness empowerment, and plant seeds for the
attainment of the vajra mind.

Finally multicolored lights then emanate from all parts of the guru's
body and enter your body from all sides. These purify subtle negative
karma collected by means of all three doors, bestow the fourth empowerment, and plant seeds for the attainment of the three inseparable vajras.

The guru visualized in front then comes to the crown of your head and dissolves into you. Your body, speech, and mind become inseparably one with the body, speech, and mind of the guru.

THE ACTUAL TANTRIC PATH

When these preliminaries have been completed you can engage in the actual tantric practices. These are of two levels: the generation stage yoga; and the completion stage yogas.

THE GENERATION STAGE YOGA

Begin by reciting the mantra of emptiness: *OM SVABHAVA SHUDDHOH SARVADHARMAH SVABHAVA SHUDDHOH HAM.* Everything dissolves into radiant emptiness.

From within the sphere of emptiness there manifests a multicolored lotus with a sun disk. Instantly you appear on it as Bhagavan Heruka Chakrasamvara, your body dark blue in color. You have four faces: the main one is black, the left one is green, the rear one is red, and the right one is yellow. Each of the faces has three eyes. You have twelve arms, and your forehead is adorned with a band of five-pointed vajras.

Your right leg is outstretched and presses down on the head of black Bhairava, who has four hands, the first two with palms joined together, the extra on the right holding a damaru drum, and the extra on the left holding a sword. Your left leg is bent in, and presses down on the breasts of red Kalarati, who also has four hands, the first two with palms joined together, the extra two holding a skull cup and a katvanga staff. Both of these supporting deities have one face and three eyes, and are adorned by the five seals.

Your first two hands embrace your consort Vajra Varahi and hold a five-pointed vajra in the right and a bell in the left. The next set of two hold the fresh, greasy skin of a white elephant, with its left foreleg in your right hand and left hind leg in your left, as though holding up a cape over your back. The fingers of your hands are formed into the threatening mudra, the hands themselves at the level of your eyebrows.

Your third right hand holds a damaru drum, your fourth a vajra axe, your fifth a vajra sword, and your sixth a trident. Your third left hand holds a katvanga staff marked by a vajra, your fourth a skull cup filled with blood, your fifth a vajra noose, and your sixth the head of Brahma, who has four faces.

Your long hair is tied up on the crown of your head and is adorned with a crossed vajra. Each of your [four] heads is adorned with a crown made of five dried human skulls and has garlands of black vajras. To the left of your crown is a shimmering half-moon crescent that emanates pacifying energies. Your four fangs [on each face] are bared and terrifying.

Your body has the three qualities of arrogance, courage, and roughness. Your speech has the three qualities of humor, force, and wrath. Your mind has the three qualities of compassion, power, and serenity. In this way you have nine vibrant presences.

You are wearing a tiger skin as a lower robe, are adorned with a necklace of freshly cut human heads strung on a string made from human gut, are sealed with the six seals, and are smeared with ashes and bone fragments from human cremation pyres.

The consort Bhagavati Vajra Varahi is gazing intensely at you, the Bhagavan. Her body is naked and is red in color. She has one face, three eyes, and two arms. Part of her hair is fixed in a knot on the top of her head and the remainder falls down loosely over her shoulders. Her right arm is wrapped around your neck and holds a skull cup filled with the blood of the four maras and other evil forces. Her right hand holds a curved knife and shows the threatening mudra to all harmful beings of the ten directions. She blazes with a fire like that at the end of time and her two legs are wrapped around your waist in order to pull you into a sexual embrace with her. Her essence is great compassion manifest in the nature of supreme bliss. She is adorned with the five seals, has a crown of five dried human skulls, and wears a belt of fifty dried human skulls.

A white syllable *OM* stands on a moon at your crown, a red syllable *AH* stands on a lotus at your throat, and a blue syllable *HUM* stands on a sun at your heart.

Lights emanate from the syllable *HUM* on the sun at your heart and summon forth Wisdom Beings that resemble you [Heruka and Consort], as well as the Initiation Deities. Make offerings to them with the mantras *OM ARGHAM PRATTICHHA SVAHA* and so forth, until *SHABTA*.

JAH HUM BAM HOH: The Wisdom Beings seem delighted and without hesitation melt into you.

Make the request to the Initiation Deities, "O Tathagatas, You Gone to Suchness, please bestow empowerment."

Having been thus requested, they sing the auspicious verse,

> Just as at the time of the Buddha's birth
> Celestial beings appeared and bathed him,
> So do we bathe you now
> With these mystical empowerment nectars.

They recite the mantra of initiation—*OM SARVA TATHAGATA ABHISHEKATA SAMAYA SHRI YE HUM*—and then pour forth empowering nectars. The nectars fill the bodies of yourself and consort and then overflow through your crown apertures. The overflow above Heruka's crown takes the form of Buddha Vajrasattva, and that above the crown of the consort takes the form of Buddha Akshobya. These become your crown ornaments. The Initiation Deities dissolve into you.

Now make the offerings to yourself manifest in the divine form of the mandala deity:

> *OM ARGHAM PRATTICHHA SVAHA*
> *OM PADYAM PRATTICHHA SVAHA*
> *OM VAJRA PUSHPE PRATTICHHA SVAHA*
> *OM VAJRA DHUPE PRATTICHHA SVAHA*
> *OM VAJRA DILIPE PRATTICHHA SVAHA*
> *OM VAJRA GENDHE PRATTICHHA SVAHA*
> *OM NAIVIDYA PRATTICHHA SVAHA*
> *OM SHABTA PRATTICHHA SVAHA*
> *OM HRIH HA HA HUM HUM PHAT.*

Male and female enter into sexual union, which gives rise to great bliss. They become utterly absorbed in the experience.

Recite the praise with the mantra *OM HRIH HA HA HUM HUM PHAT. OM VAJRA VAIROCHANI YE HUM HUM PHAT SVAHA.*

Having meditated in this way, you should now concentrate on the absorption of the divine tantric pride of sensing yourself as actually being Heruka Chakrasamvara and Consort. Remain in this meditation for as long as possible.

Then engage in the mantra recitation. Visualize that the following mantra stands in a circle around the syllable *HUM* at your heart: *OM HRIH HA HA HUM HUM PHAT.*

Recite this mantra as many times as possible, while engaging in the meditation as taught in the oral tradition.

THE COMPLETION STAGE YOGAS

There are two main practices, the first of which involves the physical exercises, together with meditating on the body as being utterly empty of materiality.

A. The Physical Exercises, Together with the Body as Empty

Within the sphere of visualizing yourself as the mandala deity, male and female in sexual union, perform the following six exercises.

In the first, which is known as "filling the body like a vase," you sit on a comfortable cushion, with your legs crossed comfortably. Your back is set straight and the hands placed on the knees.

Draw in air through the right nostril, glance to the left, and then release the air through the left, exhaling slowly and gently until no more remains in the lungs. Then draw in air through the left nostril, gaze to the right, and gently release it via the other nostril. Next draw in the air through both nostrils, glance straight ahead, and release it slowly through both. Repeat this cycle of three breaths two more times. In this way the breath is purified by means of nine cycles. With both inhalation and exhalation, no air should be allowed to pass through the mouth.

Now sit with the body straight and erect, the hands formed into fists with the thumbs inside. Breathe in slowly and deeply, and push the air down to below the navel. Swallow some saliva without making a sound and press down [on the ball of air] with the abdomen, as though the air was being pushed to a point just below the navel chakra. Simultaneously pull up air from below and contract the muscles of the pelvic floor.

Hold the breath for as long as is comfortable. As you do so, press down [with the abdomen] and pull up [with the muscles of the pelvis floor]. In this way the upper and lower airs are held in an embrace at the navel and the body is filled [with air], like water in the belly of a vase.

Imagine that your consciousness is located at the center of the navel chakra. Hold the breath as long as you can, and when it can no longer be retained, let it out slowly via the nose, without allowing any to be exhaled via the mouth.

This, the vase breathing technique, is the first of the six exercises. All of the five remaining exercises are performed while engaging in it.

The second exercise is called "circling like a wheel." Here you should sit in the vajra posture, hold the big toe of the right foot with the right hand, and the big toe of the left foot with the left hand. Straighten the spine, and roll the upper waist and stomach clockwise three times and then counterclockwise three times. Next stretch the upper body from the left to the right, and then from the right to the left. Finally snap the solar plexus from the front toward the back, and then from the back toward the front.

The third exercise is called "hooking like a hook." Form the hands into vajra fists, tense your muscles, and stretch your arms outward, beginning from your heart and reaching directly in front of your chest. Then stretch your two arms to the left, and slowly but with muscles tensed slide the right hand back to the right shoulder. Next bring the left hand to the heart, and snap the left elbow into the rib cage. Repeat this process three times.

Now do the same movement in reverse. First make the vajra fist mudra, beginning with the two hands at the heart, and then extend your arms straight outward. Do this slowly but with tensed muscles. Stretch them to the right, and hook them as before [except in reverse], bringing the left hand to the left shoulder and the right hand to the heart, and snapping the right elbow into the rib cage.

The fourth exercise is that of showing the mudra of vajra binding, lifting upward toward the sky, and then pressing downward. Plant the knees flat on the floor, straighten the body, and then, with the fingers of both hands stretched upward like metal hooks, lift upward slowly but with great intensity into the space above your head. Then reverse the hands, so that the hooked fingers point downward, and bring them down slowly but with intensity.

The fifth exercise is that of making the body straight as an arrow and then expelling the air with the sound of a dog heaving. Kneel on the floor, straighten your body, place your hands on the floor, and put your head between your hands. Slowly yet with intensity raise your head and straighten your body. Then bring your head back down to between your two hands and forcefully expel all air from the lungs. As you do this, make the sound "hah," like a dog heaving. Then stand up and shake your feet three times each.

The sixth exercise involves shaking the head and body and flexing the joints. Pull on the fingers of your two hands in order to pop the joints and then shake your head and body vigorously. Conclude by rubbing your two hands as though washing them.

It is important to hold your breath and control the vital energies when practicing these physical exercises. All movements should be slow yet intense.

The best time to engage in the exercises is either before you eat or else several hours after having eaten, when the stomach has digested most of the food. Persevere in the practice until your body becomes completely flexible.

As for the meditation on the body as being empty, here you should visualize yourself as being the mandala deity and should imagine that your entire body is utterly empty of material substance, from the tip of your head to the soles of your feet. It is like an intestine inflated with radiantly bright air. Keep your mind firmly and clearly on this image.

B. The Stages of Meditation upon the Actual Path of the Six Yogas

This involves two levels of practice: the essence of the actual path; and the branches of that path, which include the practices of consciousness transference and forceful projection.

The first of these involves two processes: arousing the four blisses by means of drawing the vital energies into the central channel; and, having accomplished that, the meditations on the illusory body and clear light yogas.[1]

The process of drawing the vital energies into the central channel and arousing the four blisses is accomplished by means of two principal techniques: the inner condition of the meditations on the inner heat yoga; and the external condition of relying upon a karmamudra.

The Inner Condition: Meditation upon the Inner Heat Yoga

Here there are two stages to the practice: meditating upon the inner heat yoga in order to draw the vital energies into the central channel; and, having brought in the energies, the methods of arousing the four blisses.

The meditation on the inner heat yoga, which draws the vital energies into the central channel, involves two stages of practice: the actual meditations on the inner heat yoga; and, having done this, the meditations that cause the vital energies to enter, abide, and dissolve within the central channel.

The actual meditation on the inner heat yoga involves three principal techniques: meditating by means of visualizing the channels; meditating by means of visualizing mantric syllables; and meditating by means of engaging in the vase breathing technique.

The first of these is the process of meditating on the inner heat by means of envisioning the channels.

Begin by imagining that in the space in front of you your root guru, together with the gurus in the line of transmission, surrounded by the host of dakas and dakinis, instantly manifest. Symbolically offer them all things good in the world and beyond. Then make the following request for blessings and realization: "May my energies be joyous. May my energy channels be subtle. And may the unique realizations of great bliss and the wisdom of emptiness be easily accomplished."

Contemplate this thought intensely, and then generate the bodhisattva resolve: "For the benefit of living beings as vast in number as the measure of the sky I will achieve the state of a Buddha Vajradhara. For this purpose I now take up the practice of *chandali*, the inner heat yoga."

Then visualize yourself as the mandala deity, sit on your meditation seat, put on your meditation belt, cross your legs, and set your backbone erect. Your neck should be bent slightly forward and your eyes cast downward at the angle of your nose. Your tongue should be held gently against your upper palate, and your teeth and lips set in their natural closed position. Posture the body and mind alertly, with the chest slightly extended. Your hands should be placed in the meditation posture just below the navel, with the back of one hand in the palm of the other.

Next you should visualize the three energy channels. The central channel, known as *avadhuti*, begins at a point four finger-widths below the navel, and runs from there up the center of the body just in front of the spinal column. To its right is the channel known as *rasana*, and to its left is *lalana*. These channels proceed up the body to the head, like pillars supporting the four chakras. The lower tips of the side channels bend into a U-shape and curve up into the base of the central channel.

Now visualize the four chakras. First at the navel is the chakra called "the wheel of emanation." Its shape is somewhat triangular, like the [Sanskrit] syllable *EH*, and it has sixty-four petals. They are red in color and stretch upward.

At the heart is the chakra known as "the wheel of truth." Its shape is somewhat circular, like the [Sanskrit syllable] *BAM*, and it has eight petals, white in color, extending downward.

At the throat is the chakra known as "the wheel of enjoyment," also somewhat circular in shape, like the syllable *BAM*. It has sixteen petals, red in color, that reach upward.

At the crown is the chakra "the wheel of great ecstasy." It also is somewhat triangular, like the syllable *EH*, and has thirty-two petals. These are multicolored and extend downward.[2]

In the beginning of the session simply place the mind on these three channels and four chakras. Meditate on both the upper and the lower regions [i.e., the two upper and two lower chakras] equally for a short period of time, and then switch your focus to the navel chakra. After that keep the mind solely on the navel chakra, which is located four finger-widths below the navel at the point inside the central channel where the three channels join, just in front of the spine.

The next step involves meditating by means of visualizing the mantric syllables. This can be done either elaborately or else simply. The elaborate method entails visualizing mantric syllables at both the center of the chakras as well as on each of the petals. The simplified practice requires visualizing only a mantric syllable at the center of each of the four chakras.

The process of this simplified technique is as follows.

First focus on the navel chakra, known as "the wheel of emana-tion." It is located inside the central channel at a point four finger-widths below the navel, just in front of the spine. At its center is an *AH*-stroke mantric syllable. This syllable stands upright upon a tiny moon disk and is in its Sanskrit form, which resembles the Tibetan character *shad* in the Tibetan classical script [i.e., the vertical stroke that divides Tibetan sentences]. It is red in color, stands upright, and is the size of a mustard seed.[3]

The heart chakra, known as "the wheel of truth," has eight petals and is located in the center of the central channel just in front of the spine at the point midway between the two nipples. At its center is a tiny moon disk, and upon it is a blue syllable *HUM*, its head pointing downward [i.e., upside down]. Meditate that it is the size of a mus-tard seed and has the power to cause the bodhimind substance to de-scend like falling snow.[4]

The throat chakra, known as "the wheel of enjoyment," has sixteen petals and is located at the center of the central channel in the throat region, just in front of the spinal column. At its center is a small moon disk with a tiny red syllable *OM* standing upright upon it, the size of a mustard seed.

The crown chakra, known as "the wheel of great bliss," has thirty-two petals and is located in the center of the central channel at the crown. At its center is a moon disk with a white syllable *HAM* standing upon it, its head pointed downward. It too is the size of a mustard seed.

All four mantric syllables are seen as having the crescent made of a half-moon, a sun, and a *nada*. Meditate that they have the power to cause the bodhimind substances to melt and fall like dew dripping from leaves, as this will intensify the force of the inner bliss that is experienced. Also, meditate that the syllables are radiantly bright, for this will cut off any mental dullness and make it easy to achieve clear concentration.

When visualizing these mantric syllables, meditate on them as though the mind has become fully blended with them. Do not do so as though looking at them from some far-off place. Holding the image either too strongly or too weakly will respectively allow mental tension or sloth to set in. It is important to focus on the image with just the right degree of force. Concentrate on the syllables in the three upper chakras for only a brief period at the beginning of each session, and then focus exclusively on the *AH*-stroke syllable at the navel chakra.

For beginners, visualizing the syllables as being very small may seem difficult. If this is the case for you, begin by envisioning them as large and then later reduce them in size.

Next meditate on the inner heat in conjunction with the vase breathing technique. Here the oral tradition of the gurus speaks of this method as having four phases: drawing in the airs; filling the stomach like the belly of a vase; compressing the airs; and releasing the airs up the central channel like an arrow.

Take care that as you draw in the airs you do not allow any breath to pass through the mouth. It should move exclusively through the nostrils. Breathe in with a strong, deep breath and then retain the airs inside, without allowing any to leave. Press the air down with the abdomen, and imagine that the air fills the two side channels, *rasana* and *lalana*. It is as though these two become completely filled, like empty intestines inflated with air.

After the side channels have become filled in this way, imagine that the air from both of the side channels flows into the central channel. Swallow without making any sound and hold your breath. Press down the upper airs to the *AH*-stroke syllable at the navel chakra and simultaneously draw in the lower airs through the two lower apertures. Direct both of these [i.e., the upper and lower airs] to the site of the *AH*-stroke mantric syllable.

In this way the upper airs are pressed down, the lower drawn up, and the two brought together in a kiss at the *AH*-stroke syllable of the navel chakra. Hold the breath for as long as possible, pushing down and pulling up respectively on the upper and lower airs as described above.

When you can no longer hold the breath, release it gently and quietly through the nostrils. Gently exhale through the nose and imagine that it comes up the central channel.

Here you should not visualize that the air leaves via the crown aperture [as some teachers advise], nor that the upper chakras, such as the heart and throat, are filled with it [as others suggest]. Instead simply concentrate on holding the airs at the *AH*-stroke mantric syllable [at the navel chakra] for as long as is comfortable.

Gradually extend the time of breath retention in a natural and unforced way. The key to success is to naturally and gently increase your power to retain the airs.

When skill in the vase breathing technique has become stabilized, engage in the method in conjunction with visualizing the four mantric syllables at the center of the chakras at the navel, heart, throat, and crown: *AM*,[5] *HUM, OM,* and *HAM.* The energies residing in the chakra at the secret place will gradually cause the *AH*-stroke syllable at the navel chakra, which is in nature the inner fire, to blaze with light and heat.

This rises up the central channel and melts the other three syllables, *HAM, OM,* and *HUM* [respectively at the crown, throat, and heart chakras]. These melt and fall into the syllable *AM* [at the navel chakra], and the four become of one inseparable nature.

At this point you should keep the mind focused on the *AM*-stroke syllable at the navel chakra, which has the nature of innate joy, and hold it there. Eventually a tiny tongue of flame from the inner heat rises up the central channel, where it melts the drop of white bodhimind substance abiding within the upper chakras. This drips down like nectar and falls into the *AM*-stroke mantric syllable at the navel chakra. Meditate single-pointedly on the *AM*-stroke, until the signs of progress arise.

Eventually your meditative stability in the practice will increase. The sign of success is that the radiance of the light from the inner fire begins to cause the inside and outside of your body, as well as your dwelling place and so forth, to seem to take on a special luster and radiance and to become as translucent as a piece of *kyurura* held in the hand.[6]

It is important during meditation sessions to keep the mind on the tiny radiant flame. This renders concentration more subtle and encourages quick and easy fulfillment of the meditative powers.

How to Cause the Energies to Enter Into, Abide, and Dissolve Within the Central Channel

Immediately after completing a practice session as described above, check the way in which the airs are flowing through your nostrils. Then engage in the bodily postures and mental applications, and after some time again observe the flow of air. Draw in several breaths in order to see how evenly the air is passing. Should it naturally flow evenly through both nostrils without any force being exerted from your side, this is a sign that the strength of the yoga has brought you to the stage wherein the energies can be drawn into the central channel.

The best sign is that, if there is no other obstruction, the airs flow through both nostrils, and the two flows are of equal strength, without one being strong and the other weak. This can be regarded as an omen that you have reached the stage at which the energies have begun to enter the central channel.

Once the energies have entered the central channel you should continue to meditate intensely. The breath will become increasingly subtle, until you will notice that it has ceased moving altogether.

Absorbing the energies into the central channel is easy for some practitioners and difficult for others. However, if you persist in the practice you will eventually begin to feel a sensation as though your solar plexus had become filled with air. The feeling may soon cease, but with persistence you will eventually feel the warmth from the residences of the inner fire in the navel and secret chakras. Fix your concentration on it. This will induce melting [of the substances] and an according experience of ecstasy.

Some practitioners are unable to achieve the signs of progress in the absorption of the energies into the central channel. This is usually a result of the fact that they have not yet eliminated subtle meditative torpor. This meditative obstacle hinders progress in the training.

For those who do not achieve proficiency in working with the energies at the center of the navel chakra, then even though they engage in the vase breathing technique and perhaps even draw the energies to the navel, the energies will not remain there and will dissipate to other sites. There is no movement of the breath, but also no retention of the energies in the desired chakra. When this is the case, there will be neither entering nor dissolving of the energies into the central channel. You should watch closely for these subtle distinctions and not mistake the stages of growth in the process.

The Manner of Inducing the Four Blisses Once the Energies Have Been Drawn Into the Central Channel

The next step in the training, once the energies have been drawn into the central channel, involves the techniques for inducing the four blisses. This is accomplished in three stages of practice: inducing the signs of success, together with igniting the inner fire; generating the four blisses by means of melting the bodhimind substances; and meditating on the innate wisdom.

The first of these three stages, that for inducing the signs of success and igniting the inner fire, begins with focusing the mind at the center of the navel chakra and bringing the life-sustaining energies into the central channel. This gives rise to five signs.

First the earth energies dissolve into those of water. There is a vision like that of a mirage of water seen in the desert heat. Next water dissolves into fire, and there is a vision like that of seeing smoke, somewhat like a vision of wispy blueness. Fire dissolves into air, and there is a vision like seeing fireflies at night, or like red sparks. Then the energies on which the conceptual mind rides dissolve, and there is a vision like that of the light of a butterlamp undisturbed by the movement of air. This energy then dissolves in four stages, each of which is likened to a sky of different colors, finally culminating in the experience of clear light consciousness. This process will be discussed later in the section on the clear light yoga, so I will not deal with it in more depth here.

Inducing the experience of these signs, such as the mirage and so forth, is not the actual method for bringing the energies into the central channel. However, working with them facilitates success in the practice. Usually they will arise in the order as described above, and be followed by the four sky-like signs.[7] When the signs arise due to the dissolutions and the process of bringing the energies into the central channel, then all five, from the mirage to the sky without clouds, will occur without interruption.

The power of the inner heat can be experienced in various ways. For example, it may arise from within the chakras at the navel and secret place and from there be brought up the central channel. It can also arise and ignite outside the central channel. This latter experience may cause some melting of the bodhimind substances, as will be explained later; but the former process is what we want to accomplish. The explanatory tantra known as *The Vajramala Tantra* puts it like this,

Energy flows through the center of all knowable things.
By awakening the inner fire, we come to experience this
    dynamic.

Also *The Mystic Kiss Tantra* states,

Moved by the karmic winds,
The mandala at the navel chakra blazes.
Know this as the supreme energy attainment.

Inducing the Four Blisses by Means of Melting the Bodhimind Drops
The descending blisses occur first as a result of the bodhimind substance located in the crown chakra being melted by the inner fire. They
drip down, and when they arrive in each of the four chakras they give
rise respectively to the four descending blisses.

When they arrive at the throat chakra, "bliss" is experienced. They
leave the throat chakra and arrive at the heart; the "supreme bliss" is
experienced. They leave the heart chakra and arrive at the navel; the
"special bliss" is aroused. Finally they leave the navel chakra and come
to the chakra at the secret place, the tip of the jewel; the "innate bliss"
is experienced.

Then the ascending blisses are aroused. Here you have to bring the
drops back up the central channel and direct them through the chakras.
As they move from the jewel chakra to the navel, "bliss" is experienced. They move from the navel to the heart, and "supreme bliss" is
induced. They move to the throat chakra, and "special bliss" is experienced. Finally, they move from the throat chakra to the crown chakra,
and "innate bliss" is aroused.

When the melting of the bodhimind substances is accomplished on
the basis of having dissolved the energies into the central channel,
then the drops can be retained at the tip of the jewel until the innate
bliss is aroused.

The drops should not be allowed to be ejaculated. This retention
will only be possible if the energy that causes ejaculation has been
absorbed [into the central channel].

In the beginning of the practice, in order to retain the drops in the
jewel chakra and arouse the innate bliss, it is useful to visualize that
the drops are directed into the central channel. Engage in the energy
practices gently until this ability is achieved. Don't overly exert force.

Eventually you will be able to bring the drops back to the crown chakra.
Correct meditation on the process of diffusing them throughout the net-

work of channels empowers you with total fluency in the process and enables you to reverse and diffuse even a great melting of the drops.

Also, if a strong experience of melting suddenly occurs and you are unable to accomplish what is described above, then revert to the visualization of yourself as being the mandala deity. Sit in the vajra posture, cross your hands in front of your chest, wrathfully elevate the gaze of your two eyes, contract the muscles of your toes and fingers, place your mind on the mantric syllable *HAM* in the crown chakra, the head of which now is seen as standing upright [unlike in the usual visualization process], and wrathfully yet slowly recite the mantric syllable *HUM* twenty-one times. Meditate that the drops are made to travel back up the central channel in front of the spine, and that they return to the crown chakra from where they descended. Then engage in a soft exercise of the vase breathing technique and also shake your body gently. Meditate that the bodhimind substances are diffused throughout the appropriate sites of your channels. Repeat this process several times.

Meditating on the Innate Wisdom

Here there are two trainings: that to be engaged during meditation sessions; and that to be engaged between meditation sessions.

Here is how to train during meditation sessions. Take the innate bliss that arises from moving the drops downward, and also the innate bliss of the ascending process, and direct it at meditation on emptiness. That is to say, at this point in the training you should engage whatever knowledge of and experience in the emptiness doctrine you have, and direct the innate bliss at it. Place the mind experiencing innate bliss in single-pointed focus on the non-inherent nature of the self and phenomena, and meditate in this way within the sphere of inseparable bliss and emptiness. Those with little experience in the emptiness doctrine should simply rest the mind in the experience of bliss. That alone is sufficient.

At the conclusion of the meditation session you arise from your meditative absorption on the innate bliss. The training in the post-meditation periods involves consciously cultivating mindfulness of the experience of bliss and emptiness conjoined. Seal all objects and events that appear and occur with the seal of bliss and emptiness. In this way the trainings in the meditation sessions and in the post-meditation periods support one another.

In brief, through practice of the inner fire yoga you unite the vital energies and invoke the four blisses. This is to be conjoined with the technique of meditating on innate bliss focused on the wisdom of emptiness.

Karmamudra, an External Condition

All the authoritative tantric scriptures and treatises point out that the practice of karmamudra is only to be performed by those who are qualified. To engage in it on any other basis only opens the door to the lower realms. The practice itself should be learned from a qualified master holding the authentic oral tradition.

The Illusory Body and Clear Light Yogas

The teaching on the illusory body and clear light yogas involves two topics. The first of these is a general discussion of how success in the inner heat yogas prepares the basis for engaging in the remaining stages of the path [i.e., the illusory body and clear light trainings]. The second is a presentation of the meditations of those two particular paths, namely the illusory body and clear light doctrines.

As for the general principles of these doctrines, here Marpa Lotsawa himself said,

> I listened to the Guhyasamaja teaching, which is a male tantra,
> And received the doctrines of the illusory body and clear light.

As Marpa points out here, the doctrines of the illusory body and clear light yogas are based upon *The Guhyasamaja Tantra*. Moreover, these doctrines are taught in detail in the Guhyasamaja tantric system known as the Arya Cycle, which is the transmission of Nagarjuna and his disciples, as elucidated in [Nagabodhi's] *An Elucidation of the Summary of the Five Stages*. As that tradition puts it, for as long as the vital energies have not been drawn into the central channel, one will not be able to generate the samadhi of the threefold experience of "appearance," "proximity," and "proximate attainment" that precedes the accomplishment of mind refinement; and it is from the state of vital energies and consciousness that have generated the complete signs of the wisdom awareness of final mind refinement that the qualified illusory body can be engaged. Similarly, the nature of the clear light doctrine should also be understood in reliance upon that same oral tradition teaching [i.e., *An Elucidation of the Summary of the Five Stages*].

Prior to the stage wherein the qualified illusory body can be made manifest one must give rise to the five signs. I discussed these in brief earlier. It would be useful at this point to explain them in a bit more detail.

The nature of the fully qualified illusory body is described in *The Five Stages*,

> The body of the yogi is transformed
> By means of the three mental states
> And the collecting of the vital energies.
> This is what is meant by "the illusory body."

This passage refers to the yogic process in which the energies of the four elements are withdrawn, giving rise to the four inner signs, such as the mirage and so forth. After that the three "inner appearances" leading up to the experience of clear light consciousness manifest.

After that has occurred, the clear light consciousness acts as the simultaneously present condition, and the life-supporting energies of the body upon which the clear light consciousness rides act as the substantial cause. This transforms the primordial bodily force into the form of a divinity, the illusory body.

Once you have produced this illusory body, it is certain that you will achieve full buddhahood in this lifetime. You discover a great space-like treasure and achieve a body-base that is immeasurable. As [Nagarjuna's] *The Five Stages* puts it,

> When one accomplishes that transformative power
> One achieves synchronicity with buddhahood itself,
> And without doubt will achieve in this very life
> The exalted state of buddhahood itself.

And also,

> One discovers an infinite space-like treasury
> Of all things required, such as dwellings, clothing, and food.
> All poverty and need is forever transcended.

Moreover, *The Guhyasamaja Tantra* states,

> The illusory body is adorned with every beauty
> And blazes with a great vajra light
> That pervades a hundred *yojanas* in distance.

The commentary known as *The Clear Lamp* [by Acharya Chandrakirti] explains that this passage means one's vajra body blazes with a great light that pervades the world for more than a hundred yojanas and is adorned with the embellishments of the thirty-two signs of perfection.

Prior to the realization of the fully characterized illusory body, you engage in the inner heat meditation in order to draw the energies into the central channel and give rise to the innate bliss. You then arouse the resolution to manifest the semblant clear light mind of utter emptiness, and by means of the energy control techniques arise in the form of a tantric deity.

This is a semblant illusory body, and its causal condition is the semblant clear light.

Based on that accomplishment you engage in the three cycles of blending with the three kayas: Dharmakaya, Sambhogakaya and Nirmanakaya.[8] This process is described in [Nagarjuna's] *The Five Stages* as follows,

> The illusory body, which is the conventional level of reality,
> Transforms into the Sambhogakaya.
> This is in the nature of the bardo experience....
>
> The ultimate level of reality, which is the clear light of mind,
> Transforms into the Dharmakaya.
> This is in the nature of the death experience.
>
> That physical form manifests as a net
> Of myriads of Nirmanakaya emanations.
> This is in the nature of the rebirth experience.

The significance of the above passages is given in *An Elucidation of the Summary of the Five Stages*, wherein it is said,

> Practice the three blendings in the bardo state.
> Practice the three blendings in the death state.
> Practice the three blendings in the rebirth state.

The "three blendings of death" are explained as follows. During the waking state one engages in the inner heat practices and gives rise to the four inner visions, known as "the four emptiness experiences." The fourth of these is the experience of clear light mind. Meditating on this clear light mind in the waking state is known as "death at the time of the path."

Then when one goes to sleep the four inner visions known as "the four emptiness experiences" naturally arise. When the fourth of these arises, which is the clear light of sleep, one meditates upon it. This is known as "death at the time of sleep."

Similarly, at the time of actual death the four inner visions known as "the four emptiness experiences" naturally arise. When the fourth of these arises, namely the clear light of death, one meditates upon it. This is known as "death at the time of death."

As for the three blendings of the bardo, these are explained as follows. During the waking state one induces the dissolutions and experiences the four emptinesses, the fourth being the clear light mind. After that, one engages the energy control techniques in order to arise in the form of a tantric deity. This is known as "the bardo of the path in the waking state."

Then when one goes to sleep and the four emptiness experiences naturally occur, the fourth being the clear light mind, one engages the energy control techniques and causes one's dream body to arise in the illusory Sambhogakaya form of the tantric deity. This is known as "the bardo of dreams in the sleep state."

Thirdly, at the time of death the elemental dissolutions naturally occur and the four emptiness experiences arise, the fourth being clear light mind. After that one enters the bardo. Here one applies the energy control techniques to cause the bardo body to transform into an illusory Sambhogakaya form of a tantric deity. This is known as "the bardo of becoming in the after-death state."

Finally, the three blendings of rebirth are as follows. During meditation sessions in the waking state one controls the vital energies and molds them into the form of a tantric deity. When one arises from this meditation and engages in activities utilizing one's ordinary body that was born from ripened karma, one does so with awareness of oneself as a tantric deity, with the Nirmanakaya aspect established at the heart. This is known as "rebirth as a path during the waking state."

During sleep one engages in the energy control practices, and in dreams transforms the dream body into a Sambhogakaya form. When one begins to awaken from dream and sleep, and to enter back into one's ordinary body formed from ripened karma, one does so with awareness of one's body being the form of a tantric deity, with the Nirmanakaya established at the heart. This is known as "rebirth at the time of awakening from dreams."

Thirdly, when one is in the after-death state and is about to take rebirth in whichever of the four ways,[9] one applies the energy control techniques and meditates on taking birth as a tantric deity, with the Nirmanakaya established at the heart. This is known as "rebirth at the time of completing the after-life."

Thus the experience of the clear light of the waking state, clear light of sleep, and clear light of death are all taken as objects of meditation and transformed into or "blended" with the Dharmakaya. Because all three are experienced after the elemental dissolutions have occurred and the four visionary states known as "the four emptiness experiences" have transpired, just as occurs naturally at the time of death, each of these three clear light experiences is termed a "death."

Similarly, the illusory body of the waking state, the illusory body of dreams, and the illusory body of the bardo are all taken as objects of meditation and are transformed into or blended with the Sambhogakaya. Because all three of these can best be understood as analogous to the bardo body that is naturally experienced after death, the name "bardo" is applied to all three.

Finally, the Nirmanakaya attained in the waking state, the Nirmanakaya meditated upon at the moment of exiting from a dream just before waking up, and the Nirmanakaya meditated upon at the completion of the bardo of death experience just before taking rebirth are best understood in relation to the manner in which one takes rebirth. Therefore each of the three is termed a "rebirth."

As for the term "blending," here the manner of blending the three clear light experiences with Dharmakaya is explained as follows. During the waking state one cultivates the ability to dissolve the energies into the central channel and bring them to the heart chakra. This gives rise to the four emptiness experiences, the fourth of which is the clear light consciousness. One remains absorbed in that clear light mind. Similarly, when one goes to sleep one engages the techniques for withdrawing the energies into the central channel at the heart chakra, and as sleep sets in one synchronizes one's meditation with the natural process of the energy withdrawals. When the fourth emptiness experience arises, which is the clear light mind of sleep, one focuses single-pointedly on it. Thirdly, one cultivates this practice throughout one's lifetime, and then when the moment of death arrives uses the familiarity that has been gained through working with the clear light minds of the waking and sleeping states. One follows the process of the withdrawal of the energies to the heart chakra and the arising of the four emptiness experiences. When the fourth of these arises, which is that of the clear light of death, one focuses on it single-pointedly, just as one had done in the waking and sleeping states.

The processes of the three blendings with Sambhogakaya and three blendings with Nirmanakaya can be understood from what is said above.

The meditation on the clear light of sleep is accomplished mainly by working with the chakras at the heart and throat. On the basis of proficiency in this yoga one is enabled to engage in an undistorted practice of the yoga of dream illusions. Approaching the practice [of dream yoga] from this perspective is indeed most praiseworthy.

The stronger one's ability to withdraw the vital energies into the central channel during the waking state, the greater will be one's success in working with the clear light of sleep. When those in whom this ability has been matured enter into sleep, they are able to work with the heart chakra in the central channel and to recognize and retain the fourth emptiness, that of the clear light of sleep. This in turn enhances their ability to work with the vital energies during the waking state and to draw them into the central channel.

Thus proficiency or lack of it in the techniques of working with the clear light of sleep greatly affects the degree of strength and efficacy of one's daytime practice and accordingly renders one's practice of this path [of the Six Yogas of Naropa] weak or strong.

Moreover, if one does not manage to achieve supreme enlightenment in this lifetime, then there is the possibility of doing so at the moment of death by means of this practice [of working with the clear light of death]. This path provides a most unique method for recognizing the clear light of death. As the moment of death approaches, one engages the techniques for retaining the clear light of death, based on the experience previously attained in the yogas of the clear light of sleep.

Similarly, in the yogas of sleep and dream one learned to recognize the clear light of sleep and then emerge in a dream body by means of recognizing the illusory body of dreams. Familiarity with that process amplified the strength of one's illusory body training during the daytime practice, and stability in the daytime practice of energy control amplified one's practice of dream yoga. If at the time of the approach of death supreme enlightenment has not been achieved, what was accomplished in the waking and sleep states can be applied at the time of death. Familiarity with the meditations of energy control and with the yoga of recognizing the clear light brought efficiency in working with the illusory dream body. That knowledge now helps in recognizing the illusory nature of the bardo experience and in transforming it accordingly.

These are the general principles upon which the illusory body and clear light doctrines are based. Next there follows a discussion of those two individual doctrines, namely the illusory body and clear light.

The main purpose of all the high tantric teachings is to point out how we can meditate on the illusory body and clear light doctrines at auspicious times in both the sleeping and waking states. The underpinnings of the training, the yogas of energy control, have already been discussed. Once this foundation has been established one should enter into the actual practice, i.e., the meditations for cultivating realization of the illusory body and the clear light.

The Illusory Body Yogas

The illusory body yogas involve three main practices: how to meditate on all appearances as illusory; how to meditate on dream illusions; and how to meditate on the illusory nature of the bardo experience.

All Appearances as Illusory

The practice here begins by examining the sense of "I" that we all have.

Examine this "I" to see if it is one with or separate from the psychophysical aggregates.[10] Eventually you will develop a firm understanding that this "I" has no self-existent nature whatsoever. This is the training on the emptiness side.

However, the conventional existence of the self arises as an object of the mind. That is to say, we have the appearance of living beings as irrefutable conventional phenomena. There are collectors of karma and experiencers of the results of karma. Even though nothing has a self-nature, all phenomena conventionally function with validity according to the laws of interdependent arising. Cultivate a definite realization of how in this way all things are ultimately empty of self-existence but nonetheless conventionally function with valid presence.

Sometimes these two levels of being may seem contradictory. To dispel this illusion, contemplate the metaphor of an image reflected in a mirror. This will generate awareness of their non-contradictory nature. Consider how the reflected image of a face, including the eyes and so forth, are empty of existing in the manner of their appearance. Based on the presence of the actual image that is being reflected, as well as the mirror and the workings of light, the reflection is created.

When one takes away the supporting conditions, such as either the face or the mirror, the image disappears. The two phenomena are interdependent.

The situation with all appearing phenomena is the same. For example, not a single particle within a living being exists to represent a final self, yet living beings collect karmic seeds, experience the results, and take rebirths according to their previously collected karmic seeds and the presence of spiritual distortions within themselves.

Appreciate the non-contradictory nature [of emptiness and relativity] in this way. As soon as you have achieved stability in this realization, extend the practice to include all objects that appear to the mind. Take all forms as manifestations of the deity; because these lack any self-existent nature, see them as illusory appearances; and see the illusions as great bliss. Train in these three awarenesses.

Meditating on Dream Illusions

This involves four trainings: learning to retain conscious presence during dreams; controlling and increasing the content of dreams; overcoming fear in dreams and training in the illusory nature of dreams; and meditating upon suchness [i.e., emptiness] in dreams.

In the first of these, retaining conscious presence during dreams, the principal method is that of the energy control that was gained by means of the inner heat yogas.

The practice begins in the waking state, during which you should cultivate the ability to bring the vital energies into the central channel and induce the experience of the four emptinesses in order to gain familiarity with the fourth emptiness, which is that of the clear light mind. Then when you go to sleep, observe the natural process of the elemental energy dissolutions and the arising of the four emptiness experiences. When the clear light of sleep arises, maintain awareness of it.

If this is done, then when dreams occur there will be no difficulty in maintaining conscious presence during them. No other method is required.

A subsidiary method involves retaining conscious presence during dreams by means of resolution. This is used by those who do not have the power of energy control and thus cannot recognize the clear light of sleep.

Here one meditates upon oneself as the mandala deity, and also meditates upon the guru and makes requests for blessings in the practice from him or her. Offer the prayer, "May I experience many dreams, may my dreams be clear and auspicious, may I retain conscious presence throughout my dreams, and may I effectively engage the special yogic applications in the dream state. May all non-conducive conditions to these ends be eliminated, and may every conducive condition manifest." You should also make *torma* offerings to the mandala deities and protector spirits, request their enlightened activity, and establish the limits of the practice place.

During the day you should continually make firm the strong resolution to be aware in the dream-state, and should combine this with the practice of repeating to yourself the thought that whatever appears is like a dream appearance and should be recognized as a dream. Also repeatedly cultivate the thought that when dreams occur you will recognize them and implement the dream yogas.

A forceful method taught in the oral tradition that is to be practiced at night is as follows. Just before going to sleep you should generate the vision of yourself as the mandala deity, with your guru seated in the space above your head. Offer intense prayers to him for blessings to succeed in the practice. Then visualize that inside the central channel at your throat chakra is a small red four-petalled lotus, with a small red mantric syllable *OM*, in nature the vajra speech, standing upon it. Maintain this visualization with clarity, not allowing the mind to lose it, and fall asleep within the sphere of retaining it.

With this technique if you still fail to retain conscious presence in your dreams, you should intensify your practice of energy control as explained earlier. If you are still unable to succeed, then remember that sleep is lightest following the period of dawn until after the sun has risen above the eastern mountains, and consequently it is easiest to accomplish dreams at that time. Therefore engage the practice at that time. Perform guru yoga, offer many prayers, and intensify the strong intent to recognize dreams when they occur. Visualize yourself as the tantric deity and imagine that there is a radiant white drop, the size of a mustard seed, between your eyebrows. Place the mind on it, perform the vase breathing technique seven times, and then go back to sleep.

If you are unable to sleep well, or your sleep is too light or is disturbed, you should cultivate conscious resolution during the day as described earlier. Then when you get ready to sleep imagine a black drop at the center of your vajra jewel chakra. Place the mind on it for some time, and then unite the vital energies twenty-one times [through vase breathing]. Within that sphere, and without letting the mind stray, drop off to sleep.

The second level of the dream yoga training involves controlling and increasing the content of your dreams. Here you can engage in various transformative exercises, such as consciously initiating a particular dream pattern or else transforming the nature of the dream altogether. Alternatively, you can project yourself on the rays of the sun or moon to a celestial realm, such as the Thirty-three Heaven, or to a faraway human realm, and see what is there. You should train in all the various activities, such as going to places, flying through the sky, and so forth.

You can also engage in visionary travel by projecting yourself to the various buddhafields, such as Sukhavati, Tushita, Akanishta, and so forth. There you can meet with the buddhas and bodhisattvas, venerate them, listen to their teachings, and engage in many other activities of this nature.

As for the exercise of "increasing the contents of dreams," this refers to increasing the number of whatever appears in the dream. Whether the dream-objects are sentient beings such as humans or animals, or inanimate objects such as pillars or vases, you simply multiply them from one to two, from two to four, and so on, until hundreds and even thousands of the object appear.

The third level of dream yoga practice is that of overcoming fear in dreams and training in the illusory nature of dreams. Here, whenever anything of a threatening or traumatic nature occurs in a dream, such as drowning in water or being burned by fire, recognize the dream as a dream and ask yourself, "How can dream water or dream fire possibly harm me?" Make yourself jump or fall into the water or fire in the dream. Examine the water, stones or fire, and remind yourself of how even though that phenomenon appears to the mind, it does not exist in the nature of its appearance. Similarly, all dream phenomena appear to the mind but are empty of an inherently existent self-nature. Meditate on all dream objects in this way.

You should train in seeing dream phenomena in this way and then in transforming the dream world and its inhabitants into the supporting and supported mandala [i.e., residence and deities].

This training also includes seeing all that is experienced in dreams as being empty of a true self-nature yet manifesting as illusory appearances. Cultivate the vision of how all phenomena are a drama of bliss and void: all appearances arise as mandala and deities, these arise as illusions, and these illusions arise in the nature of the wisdom of bliss and emptiness.

The fourth level of the dream yoga training is that of meditating upon the suchness of dreams. This stage of the practice can only be undertaken when the training in retaining conscious presence during dreams has become stable. Here meditate upon yourself as the manifest radiant form of the mandala deity. The mantric syllable *HUM* shines with a great light from your heart. This light melts the animate and inanimate dream objects into light, which is absorbed into yourself. Your body then also melts into light, from the head downward and feet upward, and is absorbed into the *HUM* at your heart. The *HUM* then melts into unapprehendable clear light. Rest the mind unwaveringly within this light.

The Illusory Nature of the Bardo

This doctrine is taught under two headings: the qualifications of the beings who can practice the bardo yogas; and the nature of the practice.

The beings who can practice the bardo yogas are said to be of three types: best, medium, and least. The qualifications of the best candidates are described in [Aryadeva's] *A Compendium of Tantric Experiences*. As that text puts it, the best practitioners are thoroughly familiar with the process of energy control, the elemental dissolutions, the experience of the four emptinesses, and so forth. At the time of death they are able to follow the natural dissolution of the elemental energies all the way to the arising of the clear light mind of death, and in the bardo can transform the illusory bardo body into the illusory body of the third stage.[11] From there they can achieve complete buddhahood in the bardo.

The qualities of medium candidates for the practice are described in *A Compendium of Tantric Experiences* as follows,

> They apply themselves just as they had done in the yogas of sleep and dream, following the process of the dissolutions, and experiencing the states known as mind, thought, and unknowing. For a moment they lose awareness, and then emerge in the unfabricated clear light consciousness. At that time the vital energies move, and they dream....

The meaning is that the medium candidate for the practice has developed the ability during his or her lifetime to recognize the four emptinesses of sleep, to apply the techniques of energy control when dreams arise, and thus to engage in dream yoga.

The principle here is that if one is able to recognize the clear light of sleep during one's lifetime practice, then at the time of death one will be able to recognize the clear light of the moment of death. Moreover, if one is able to control the subtle energies in the dream state, one will be able to control them in the bardo. When the clear light of death arises one will recognize it; and when this clear light passes and one enters into the bardo, one will be able to recognize the bardo experience, control the subtle energies within it, and effect the desired transformations.

Candidates regarded as having the least qualification for practicing the bardo yogas are those who are stable in guarding the tantric commitments and have made some progress in the generation and completion stage yogas. At the time of death they maintain whatever awareness they can throughout the process of the elemental dissolutions, beginning with the earth energies dissolving into those of water, and so forth, up to the emergence of the clear light mind of the moment of death. The clear light passes and they emerge into the bardo. Although they have not developed fluency in the waking state practices of energy control, nor the power of sleep and dream yogas, they are sufficiently well versed in the oral transmission teachings and are able to recollect them at that important moment. Thus they engage in the bardo yogas on the strength of previous familiarity with the oral tradition teachings.

As for the nature of the practice for these three types of candidates, here the best trainees simply recognize the nature of the bardo body and then transform it into a Sambhogakaya form.

For medium candidates, when the time of death comes they should maintain a clear state of mind and distribute all their belongings and possessions to worthy recipients in order to eliminate any grasping or attachments. Then they should consciously acknowledge to themselves any transgressions of their practice guidelines and commitments that occurred during their lifetime, as well as any general spiritual failings, and purify and renew these. For their meditation, they should visualize themselves as the mandala deity and envision the guru and host of mandala deities as coming into their presence. Then they should make offerings and forcefully and repeatedly offer the prayer, "Grant blessings that I may be able to effect the blending of the clear light of death. Grant blessings that I may be able to effect the blending of the illusory bardo body."

[At the time of death, certain] external and internal signs of the energy dissolutions occur. First the earth element dissolves into the water element. The external sign is that one loses the ability to move one's limbs or control the body, and one has an appearance of total relaxation. There is a sensation as though one's body were sinking into the earth. The inner sign is a vision having a mirage-like quality. Next the water element dissolves into the fire element. The external sign is dryness of mouth and nose and a shrivelling of the tongue. The inner sign is a vision as though of smoke. The fire element now dissolves into the air element. The external sign is that one's body heat begins to drop, withdrawing from the extremities [toward the heart]. The inner sign is a vision like that of seeing sparks or of seeing a cluster of fireflies.

Next the air element of conceptual thought dissolves into mind. Here the vital energies that support conceptual thought dissolve into consciousness. The external sign is that a long breath is exhaled and the body seems unable to inhale. Even if one can inhale, one does so shallowly yet heavily. The inner sign is a vision of a light resembling that of a butterlamp undisturbed by wind movement.

After this the first emptiness occurs, known simply as "emptiness." This is the experience of the vision known as "appearance." The inner sign is of whiteness, like seeing moonlight in a cloudless sky. The consciousness of "appearance" then dissolves into the second emptiness, known as "very empty." This is the experience of the vision known as "proximity." The inner vision is of a yellowish red light, like that of the light at sunrise. This dissolves into the third emptiness, "the great emptiness," which is linked to the experience of the vision known as "proximate attainment." The inner vision is of utter darkness, like that of a night sky pervaded by thick darkness. The person has a sensation of swooning and loses consciousness. After this the person emerges from the darkness and the state of mindlessness, and arises into the experience of "utter emptiness," also termed "the clear light." The vision is of a color like the blending of the lights of sun and moon in a sky free from all darkness, like the clear sky at early dawn. This is the clear light that is the actual basis.

One should understand the stages of these elemental dissolutions and be aware of them as they occur. As each of the four signs manifests, such as the mirage and so forth, one should contemplate how neither the self nor phenomena have any true existence whatsoever. Again, as the experiences of the four emptinesses manifest, together with the visions of a cloudless sky pervaded by moonlight, and so forth, one meditates on how neither the self nor phenomena have any true existence. Especially, when the fourth emptiness manifests with the sign of a cloudless sky, which is the clear light mind in which the coarse sense of duality is pacified, one attempts to recognize and remain in meditation on it for as long as possible.

Jetsun Milarepa stated, "The clear light of death is the Dharmakaya; one only must recognize it as such. In order to be able to do so, one should be introduced to it now by a supreme master. Cultivate an understanding of the essence of the view of the way things are, and train in the symbolic clear light of the path."

Here the words "symbolic clear light of the path" refer to the experience of the clear light consciousness on the two occasions: that which arises as the fourth emptiness experience as a result of tantric practice in the waking state [i.e., the clear light consciousness invoked through the inner fire yogas]; and that which is known as the fourth emptiness experience of the sleep process [i.e., the clear light of sleep].

The practitioner should conjoin the practice of the bardo yoga with a firm resolution by retaining the thought, "As soon as I pass through the fourth emptiness of the death experience and enter into the bardo, I will arise in the illusory bardo body as my mandala deity."

The ability to succeed in this practice very much depends upon the familiarity with the illusory body trainings that was accomplished during one's lifetime in the twofold practice of the illusory body of the waking state and the illusory body of dreams. The principle here is that when one is in the bardo one engages the same type of meditations that were previously cultivated—the waking state practice of seeing all appearances as an illusion and the dream-time practice of observing dream illusions.

The practice here involves taking everything that manifests in the bardo experience and transforming it into the supporting and supported mandalas by means of one's meditation. One contemplates how all the things that appear are empty of true existence, yet nonetheless manifest in an illusory manner as real phenomena; and one observes how the illusory appearances arise in the nature of inseparable bliss and emptiness.

You can also make a strong aspiration to be reborn in a buddhafield. Alternatively, if you are in possession of the instructions on consciousness transference, you can apply these techniques at this point.

These are the methods to be utilized by the practitioner of medium qualification.

The third type of practitioners [i.e., the least qualified] should try to proceed in much the same way as did the medium practitioner described above. Should they have the good fortune to pass away in a clear state of mind, they should without any regrets distribute all their belongings and possessions to worthy recipients, consciously acknowledge to themselves any transgressions of their practice guidelines and commitments that occurred during their lifetime, as well as any general spiritual failings, and then purify and renew these.

Then they should visualize themselves as the mandala deity, meditate that the guru and host of mandala deities come into their presence, offer devotions to them, and forcefully and repeatedly offer the following prayer, "Grant blessings that I may be able to effect the blending of the clear light of death. Grant blessings that I may be able to effect the blending of the illusory bardo body."

Practitioners who are in this category should not wait until death befalls them to begin the bardo yoga. During their lifetime they should continually strive to familiarize themselves with the signs of the four elemental dissolutions and four emptiness visions, and cultivate the habit of observing how the self and phenomena are empty of true existence yet manifest as illusions. They should make a strong resolution that after the clear light of death passes they will gain realization in the bardo, and they should meditate on the three circles: how everything manifests as illusions, how the illusions manifest as supported and supporting mandalas, and how these arise in the nature of bliss and emptiness.

This practice should be coupled with the strong aspiration to achieve rebirth in a buddhafield.

The Clear Light Yogas
Training in the clear light doctrines involves two main practices: how to train in the waking state; and how to train in the clear light of sleep.

Working With the Clear Light of the Waking State
The actual practice of the clear light yogas is intended for those who have achieved the basis of a qualified illusory body experience or a proxy of it.

Here visualize yourself as the mandala deity, male and female in sexual union. The "wheel of truth" chakra is at your heart with the central channel running through it. A blue mantric syllable *HUM* stands on a sun disk located there.

Lights emanate from this and purify the inanimate universe. The universe melts into clear light, which absorbs into the animate universe. These then melt into clear light and into yourself as the mandala deity. The female aspect melts into the male of the mandala deity.

Then from your crown downward and feet upward you melt into light, which is absorbed into the syllable *HUM* at your heart.

The syllable *HUM* then melts into light from the bottom upward, beginning with the *U* vowel underneath melting into the *AH*, that into the *HA*, that into its head, that into the crescent moon above, that into the drop, and that into the *nada* above it.

In this way everything is absorbed into the center of the central channel at the heart chakra. Hold your mind firmly there.

Meditating in this way for a prolonged period will eventually induce the experiences of the four emptinesses, the fourth of which is the "waking-state clear light of the path." Without wavering, place awareness on it.

The methods for cultivating the clear light are taught in detail in the *Guhyasamaja Tantra*.

Working With the Clear Light of Sleep

Just as proficiency in the waking state yogas of energy control is the supreme condition for success in the practice of working with dreams, so again here energy control is the best qualification for someone who wishes to engage in the process of working with the clear light of sleep.

The practice as transmitted in the instructions of the lineage gurus is explained as follows.

Begin by making offerings to the Three Jewels, perform *torma* offerings to the Dharma Protectors, and send forth the prayer, "May I recognize the clear light of sleep, and may all obstructions to success in the practice be eliminated." Meditate on yourself as being the mandala deity, meditate on guru yoga, and send forth many prayers for blessing power to assist in the effort to retain the clear light of sleep. Generate a strong resolution that you will not slip into dreams, but instead will recognize the four emptinesses of sleep.

As you prepare to go to sleep, lie on your right side in the posture of the sleeping lion,[12] with your head to the north, face to the west, and your right arm tucked underneath your body. Visualize yourself as the mandala deity and envision a blue four-petalled lotus at your heart chakra, the central channel running through it, a blue mantric syllable *HUM* at its center. Meditate upon this syllable as though your mind had become utterly blended with it and then go to sleep.

If during the waking state you have cultivated the ability to induce the experience of the four elemental dissolutions and four emptinesses by means of the inner heat yoga, then doing the above practice at the time of going to sleep will produce the desired results. The energies will enter the central channel and you will recognize the clear light of sleep.

Some practitioners lack the ability to draw the energies into the central channel and induce the experience of the four emptinesses during the waking state. They should apply a general samadhi free from torpor and on that basis at the time of going to sleep should engage in the meditations explained above. Alternatively, during the waking state they can cultivate that samadhi and then when going to sleep can direct it in mindfulness of the dissolution process.

However, the clear light of sleep experienced in this way will not be the fully qualified clear light as described in the tantric treatises. Even if the samadhi is directed at awareness of the view of suchness, it will still only be an experience of the clear light as taught on the common path. It is not the clear light consciousness induced by highest yoga tantra.

The techniques for working with the clear light of sleep are discussed in detail in [Aryadeva's] *A Compendium of Tantric Experiences*.

Next follows a discussion of the auxiliary practices of the Six Yogas path, namely, the yogas of consciousness transference and forceful projection.

The Yoga of Consciousness Transference

The oral tradition of the gurus teaches the practice of consciousness transference yoga as follows.

Visualize yourself as the mandala deity and bring the vital energies into a kiss at either the secret place or the navel chakra. Imagine a red *AH*-stroke syllable at the navel chakra, a dark blue *HUM* at the heart chakra, and a white *KSHA* at the crown aperture.

Now pull up forcefully on the vital energies from below. These strike the *AH*-stroke syllable at the navel chakra, which rises and strikes the *HUM* at your heart. This rises and strikes the *KSHA* at your crown.

Then reverse the process. Pull the *HUM* back down to the heart chakra, and the *AH* back down to the navel chakra.

Apply yourself to this training until the signs of accomplishment manifest. These include phenomena such as a small blister appearing on the crown of the head, a sensation of itching, and so forth.

When the time comes for the actual application [i.e., at the time of death], place the body in the *tsig-bu* position, with the two arms wrapped around the knees. Take refuge in the Three Jewels, generate the universalist bodhisattva attitude, and then meditate upon yourself as being the mandala deity.

From within this sphere visualize your root guru, in aspect inseparable from [i.e., appearing in the form of] your meditational deity. He manifests in the space in front of your forehead and is roughly an armspan or half an armspan in distance from you. Offer strong heartfelt prayers to him.

Then focus on the three mantric syllables: the red *AH*-stroke at your navel chakra; the blue *HUM* at your heart chakra, and the white *KSHA* at your crown. Pull up forcefully on the energies from below. This causes the *AH*-stroke syllable to spin up the central channel from the navel chakra. It melts into the *HUM* at the heart chakra. Recite the mantra *AH-HIK* many times. The *HUM* syllable moves up the central channel. Recite the mantra *AH-HIK* twenty-one times; this causes it to continue up to the throat chakra.

Turn your attention to the syllable *KSHA* at the mouth of the Brahma aperture [at the crown]. It is as though silhouetted against a background of pure white sky-like light, like an object in a roof window. Recite *AH-HIK* forcefully five times. This causes the syllable *HUM* to shoot out the Brahma aperture and melt into the heart of the guru inseparable from the mandala deity. Rest the mind there in the state of beyond-conceptuality awareness.

This is the method taught by the gurus of the lineage.

The sixth and final yoga is that of forceful projection of consciousness into another body. I will not deal with it here, as it is an extremely secret practice.[13]

This completes my compilation of the quintessential instructions on how to take into one's hands the stages of visualization and meditation associated with the profound path known as the Six Yogas of Naropa.

> O hark! May the light rays of the two stages of tantric practice
> Shine forth like waves of life-giving ambrosia,
> Eliminating all darkness and suffering that exists
> And causing the flowers of joy and freedom to bloom.

6

The Golden Key:
A Profound Guide to
the Six Yogas of Naropa

Tib. *Na ro'i chos drug gi zab 'khrid gser gyi sde mig*

by

Panchen Lobzang Chokyi Gyaltsen
the First Panchen Lama

1568–1662

Translator's Preamble

Panchen Lobzang Chokyi Gyaltsen was one of the greatest lamas of seventeenth-century Tibet. During his lifetime he was informally regarded as the reincarnation of a number of important Gelukpa monks, including Gyalwa Wensapa, the author of the text translated in Chapter Four. However, he was never enthroned as a reincarnate, but simply rose to his position of greatness due to his personal spiritual charisma, his talents as a teacher, and his popularity as a writer.

Panchen Lobzang Chokyi Gyaltsen served as the tutor to the young Fifth Dalai Lama, and after the Fifth Dalai Lama became the spiritual and temporal leader of Tibet in 1642 he showed great respect to his guru. He gave him Tashi Lhunpo, the monastery that had been built by the First Dalai Lama two centuries earlier, with the instruction that his future incarnations should be enthroned and educated there. Thus Tashi Lhunpo Monastery became the hereditary seat of the subsequent Panchen Lamas, and this is still the case today. The Seventh Panchen Lama passed away in 1989 in Tashi Lhunpo.[1]

From that time until the present century the Panchen and Dalai Lamas have been known in Tibetan as Yab Sey (Tib. *yab sres*), or "Father and Son," with whichever of the two is the older serving as the guru to the younger in their subsequent string of reincarnations.

Jey Sherab Gyatso, the author of the text translated in Chapter Three, commented,

> The two most clear and concise manuals on the manner of meditating on the inner heat are those by the Second Dalai Lama, Gyalwa Gendun Gyatso, and the First Panchen Lama, Panchen

Chogyen. One should meditate in accordance with their instructions, for they present the tradition embodied in Tsongkhapa's *A
Book of Three Inspirations* in a most wonderful and practical manner.

The present chapter contains a translation of the second of these two
works, that by Panchen Chokyi Gyaltsen, or, as Jey Sherab Gyatso
calls him, Panchen Chogyan, "Ornament of the Dharma."

Jey Sherab Gyatso recommends it for its treatment of the inner heat
yoga. However, it is perhaps even more important for its treatment of
powa, or the yoga of consciousness transference at the time of death,
as it goes into this practice in considerable detail. Because this yoga is
applied at the time of death, I have placed this work at the end of this
collection.

The Golden Key:
A Profound Guide to
the Six Yogas of Naropa

by Panchen Lobzang Chokyi Gyaltsen

Homage to Manjushri, the Bodhisattva of Wisdom.

I bow to the illustrious spiritual masters,
Who emanate forth in a vajra dance of enlightenment's union
From the sphere of great bliss inseparable from unfabricated
profound wisdom
And bring every supreme goodness to living beings.
In respect to them I herein set forth
This treatise on the essence of the Six Yogas instruction.

THE PRELIMINARY TRAININGS

Those who wish to enter into the practice of the tradition everywhere
famed as the Six Yogas of Naropa should begin by training their minds
in the common paths [i.e., the Sutrayana methods].[2] After that they
should receive the four complete initiations into an appropriate
anuttara-tantra system, such as either Chakrasamvara or Hevajra. *The
Mark of Mahamudra* states,

> Without empowerment there will be no attainment,
> Just as oil does not come from pressing sand.

As said here, one should receive the appropriate empowerments before entering into tantric practice. In addition, one should then guard the precepts and commitments taken at the time of initiation, just as one would guard one's life. *The Root Tantra of Heruka Chakrasamvara* states,

> The practitioner engaged in intense tantric training
> Should constantly maintain the tantric precepts.
> If the precepts become weakened,
> No siddhi is achieved from initiation into the mandala.

Thus the trainee receives initiation, guards the precepts and commitments of the tantric path, and then takes up the mandala meditations of the generation stage yogas. The generation stage practice should embody the complete process of taking the three occasions—death, intermediate state and rebirth—as the three enlightenment kayas: Dharmakaya, Sambhogakaya, and Nirmanakaya.[3] Arya Nagarjuna put it this way,

> Firstly establish yourself well in the generation stage yogas
> And then aspire to the completion stage yogas.
> This is the method taught by the Buddha.
> These [two yogas] are like the steps of a ladder.

All highest yoga tantra systems are similar in this respect. They all advocate accomplishing maturity in the generation stage mandala meditations before entering into the completion stage practices.

The early masters in the Six Yogas tradition also advocated several special preparatory trainings: meditating on refuge and bodhisattva perspective; the Vajrasattva meditation and mantra recitation; and the practice of guru yoga, together with the mandala offering. One should engage in these with intense feelings of devotion and supplication for blessings.[4]

THE ACTUAL PRACTICE

Although there are various ways of categorizing the methods taught in the Six Yogas, *The Vajra Song of the Six Yogas of Naropa*[5] speaks of them as follows: inner heat; illusory body; clear light; consciousness transference; the bardo yogas; and projection into another residence. These six embody the essence of both the male and female tantras.

Jey Marpa Lotsawa sang the following verse,

> At the feet of the gatekeeper, the mighty Pandita Naropa,
> I listened to the profound tantric teachings of the Hevajra
>   system.

There I received the precepts on blending, transference, and
  union.
In particular, I received the instructions
On inner heat yoga and the practice of karmamudra,
And was introduced to the key points of the whispered
  tradition.

As stated above, the teachings on the inner heat yoga in the Six Yogas
tradition are derived from the *Hevajra Tantra*, which is a female tantra
system. Elsewhere Marpa sang,

In the west, in the town of Tulakshetra,
I bowed at the feet of the glorious Jnanagarbha
And listened to the *Guhyasamaja Tantra*, a male tantric system.
There I received the instructions on the illusory body and clear
  light
And trained in the essence of the five stages of the path.[6]

Thus Marpa himself states that the illusory body and clear light yogas
are derived from the *Guhyasamaja Tantra*, which is a male tantra system.
   Finally, the yogas of consciousness transference and projection into
another residence are based on *The Chaturpita Tantra* and *The Mystic
Kiss Tantra*.
   [Nagabodhi's] *Elucidation of the Summary of the Five Stages* states,

By means of the inner heat energy yogas,
Great bliss arises as the force of the mind.

The meaning of this passage is that one engages in the yogas of energy control, such as the vajra breath repetition and so forth as taught
in the *Guhyasamaja Tantra* and other such systems, until eventually the
experience of the clear light consciousness known as "final mind isolation" is induced. This achievement depends upon one first achieving proficiency in the inner heat yoga as taught in the Hevajra and
Chakrasamvara systems, by means of which one induces the four
blisses—both the four descending[7] and four ascending blisses—and
thus induces the experience of the semblant clear light consciousness
that arises together with the innate bliss.
   This is the case in both the Six Yogas of Naropa and the Six Yogas of
Niguma. Therefore in both of these traditions it is said that the inner
heat yoga is the foundation stone and life-tree of all the completion
stage practices.
   Jey Naropa sang a song to Marpa Lotsawa,

The manner of approaching the nature of the mind
Is to meditate upon the principle of emptiness;
The manner of approaching the nature of the body

Is to meditate from within the following perspective:
All outer and inner illusions arise as the deity's illusory body;
Inside the body are three channels and four chakras;
Below is the *AH*-stroke syllable representing the *chandali* inner
    heat,
And above is the *HAM* syllable.
There is blazing [of the fires] and dripping [of the drops];
The energies swirl above and below.
In between, radiant bliss and emptiness are experienced.
The name of this is the inner heat yoga.
O Lotsawa, have you experienced the mind from this perspective?

Anyone who wishes to engage in the inner heat yogas should take
up residence in a quiet and pleasant place. Sit on a meditation cushion
in the seven-point posture, or else wear a meditation belt and sit with
legs crossed accordingly. Begin the session by clarifying the breath
and bodily energies.[8] Then meditate on guru yoga as a preliminary,
recite verses of refuge to the spiritual master, and then offer strong
prayers that your energies may remain blissful and energy channels
supple, and that you may give rise to special realization of blissful
inner heat.

As a final preliminary, generate the bodhisattva motivation by meditating on the thought, "For the benefit of all living beings I will achieve
complete buddhahood in this very lifetime, and for this purpose now
enter into meditation on the inner heat yoga." Meditate in this way
until your mindstream becomes totally infused with the bodhisattva
aspiration.

When these preliminaries have been completed, generate the vision of yourself either as Vajrayogini, with your body red in color, or
else as Heruka Chakrasamvara, with your body as blue as lapis lazuli.
Envision your form as being utterly empty of substance, like an inflated
balloon. It is both transparent and radiant, like a rainbow in the sky.

Inside one's body are the three energy channels. Firstly one visualizes the central channel, known as *avadhuti*. It runs up and down the
center of the body just in front of the spine, and resembles a somewhat large and hollow wheat straw or reed. As for the color of this
energy channel, *The Samputa Tantra* states that when the inner heat is
being ignited it should be seen as being the color of the flame of a
lamp burning sesame seed oil; before the inner fire has been aroused,
however, it should be seen as being light blue.

To its right is the channel *rasana*, which is red in color, and to its left
is the channel *lalana*, white in color. They begin at a point four

finger-widths below the navel and run upward toward the crown in the manner of a central pillar supporting the house of the body.

At their base the two side channels curve and flow into the central channel. Located at that point is the multicolored navel chakra, known as "the wheel of emanation," with sixty-four channel petals.

At the heart the channels form a knot, and there one envisions "the wheel of truth" chakra, white in color, with eight channel petals. Again at the throat they form a knot, and there one visualizes "the wheel of enjoyment" chakra, red in color, having sixteen channel petals. Finally again at the crown they form a knot, and there one visualizes "the wheel of great bliss" chakra, white in color, having thirty-two channel petals.

The Samputa Tantra states,

> The chakras at the crown and navel
> Are triangular in shape, like the Sanskrit syllable *EH.*
> The chakras at the throat and heart are in between them,
> And are circular in shape, like the Sanskrit syllable *VAM.*

The meaning is that the two sets represent method and wisdom combined, just as does the Sanskrit word *E-vam.*

Their shape is such that the petals of the navel chakra flow upward and those of the heart chakra flow downward, as though the two chakras are reaching out to embrace one another. Similarly, those of the throat chakra flow upward, and those of the crown chakra flow downward, as though reaching toward one another in an embrace.

This manner of visualizing the three energy channels and four chakras is in accordance with the teaching of the Indian mahasiddha Lawapa, and is the technique advocated [by Lama Tsongkhapa] in *A Book of Three Inspirations.*

After this one places the mantric syllables in the chakras. This is done as taught in the Hevajra Tantra.

Here one focuses the mind at the very center of the central channel at the sites of the four chakras. At each of these, standing on a moon cushion the size of a small pea cut in half, is a mantric syllable.

At the crown chakra is a white syllable *HAM,* its head pointed downward [i.e., standing upside down]; at the throat chakra is a white *OM,* its head pointed upward; at the heart is a blue or mercury-colored *HUM,* its head pointed downward; and at the navel is the *AH*-stroke syllable, its head pointed upward.

All four of these syllables are the size of mustard seeds, and all have their heads adorned with a crescent made of the three symbols: a half moon, a drop, and a *nada* [zigzag line].

The nadas on the syllables *AH* and *OM* [which are standing upright] are hot and red, as though about to burst into flame. From the nadas of the other two syllables [which are standing upside down] bodhimind substances drip down, like dewdrops falling from above, or like small spiders descending down from their threads.

Envision all these syllables as being intensely bright. Keep the mind fixed firmly on them. Avoid the two obstacles of mental torpor and agitation, and meditate on them single-pointedly.

In general you should focus your attention on all four syllables, although in the early stages of practice you should pay special attention to the *AH*-stroke syllable at the navel.

When familiarity with this meditation has produced stability in the practice, engage in the vase breathing technique in rotation. The manner of doing so is as follows.

First turn your attention to the point below the navel chakra where the two side channels curve into the central channel. Then observe the upper sites of the channels, and how the central channel comes to a point between the [upper apertures of your] nostrils, with the two side channels terminating at the [upper apertures of the] nostrils.

The vase breathing is then done in four stages: inhaling, filling, dissolving, and releasing like an arrow.

Here the breath is not inhaled through the mouth, but is drawn in gently through the two nostrils. This is the first step. Secondly the two side channels are seen as becoming completely filled, like balloons inflated with air. Thirdly the air in the two side channels is seen as entering into the central channel. It dissolves into the *AH*-stroke syllable slowly, until the two side channels are emptied. The dissolution is gradual, like water poured onto sand slowly is absorbed into the sand. This is the process of dissolving.

At this point in the technique one swallows, and presses down with the upper energies while gently pulling up the lower energies from below. Both [upper and lower energies] dissolve into the *AH*-stroke syllable. Meditate that mind and energy become inseparably one with the *AH*-stroke syllable. *The Arising of Samvara Tantra* states,

> The energies that course above and below
> Through the mind are brought to a kiss.

Retain the breath and energies in this way [at the navel chakra] for as long as discomfort does not set in. Then release the breath gently through the nostrils, visualizing that the energies rise and swirl up the central channel. This is the fourth step, called "releasing like an arrow."

As this yoga becomes stable the power of the inner heat is gradually ignited. The syllables at the heart and throat are melted and scorched, and the *HAM* syllable at the crown begins to drip bodhimind drops, which descend through the chakras.

In this way the *AH* and *HAM* respectively blaze and drip, giving rise to the four blisses in consecutive and then reverse orders [i.e., descending and ascending], until eventually great bliss is aroused.

This mind of great bliss is then focused single-pointedly in meditation upon emptiness. The mind and energies are repeatedly brought to one point in this way, and the energies are directed to the mouth of the central channel and caused to enter, abide and dissolve, until eventually the consciousness of the semblant clear light manifests.

One abides in this semblant clear light, and when the time comes to arise from it one sets the resolve to arise in the form of Heruka and Consort in sexual union. In this way one enters back into the coarse aggregates, seeing them as a Nirmanakaya with the Jnanasattva[9] at one's heart, and cultivates the between-sessions yoga.

In case the yogi is not able to achieve complete realization of all the stages leading to enlightenment before death arrives, he or she meditates on the *HUM* at the heart in the sleeping state and uses this for preparing for the death experience, meditating single-pointedly upon the clear light of sleep and the illusory nature of dreams. This is the practice known as "blending sleep experience and death experience."

Practicing in this way, engage the blending of the three kayas in both waking and sleeping states.

When the practice has developed stability and you have arrived at the point where the knots constricting the heart chakra are ready to be released, take up the practice of karmamudra with a qualified sexual consort, with you being the relier and the consort being the relied-upon, until the energies that support the final semblant clear light arise in the actual form of Heruka. [Nagarjuna's] *The Five Stages* describes the experience thus,

> The illusion-like samadhi
> Perceives everything in that way.

The meaning of this passage is that the illusory samadhi is taken to complete fulfillment.

The illustrious Naropa said to Marpa Lotsawa,

> Day and night appearances manifest as illusory forms;
> This is the instruction known as "the illusory body."
> Have you reversed all grasping at appearances, O Lotsawa?

The practitioner takes the illusory yoga to fulfillment, and eventually perceives the signs of the eradication of all spiritual distortions, together with their seeds. He or she relies on the inner conditions of the energy yogas and the outer conditions of a sexual consort, and thus causes the inner and outer signs of enlightenment to manifest. This is the experience of the actual clear light. Jey Naropa sang to Marpa Lotsawa,

> In the space between sleep and dreams
> Is unknowing, in nature the Dharmakaya.
> It is to be drawn into one's experience
> As inexpressible, uncontrived emptiness.
> Thereafter, whatever appears arises as bliss.
> This is the unfabricated primordial nature of being
> And is called "the clear light instruction."
> Have you fathomed this unborn mind, O Lotsawa?

From the uncontaminated energy and consciousness that support this mind of actual clear light arises the vajra body of great union, on the basis of which the resultant state of full buddhahood in the form of a Vajradhara endowed with the seven excellent qualities is achieved.

THE AUXILIARY TRAININGS

Thus in the tradition of the Six Yogas of Naropa it is said that the main practices are those of the inner heat, illusory body, and clear light yogas; the remaining three yogas—consciousness transference, forceful projection into another body, and the bardo yogas—are but branches of the path.

The idea is that if one is not able to accomplish all the practices leading to enlightenment before death comes to destroy one's body-vessel, then in order to fulfill the purposes of oneself and others one engages the yogas of either consciousness transference or projection into another body. Alternatively, if one is unable to effect this transference, or if one wishes instead to attempt to accomplish final enlightenment in the bardo, then there is the doctrine of the bardo yogas.

From among these three, these days it is most important to know the consciousness transference yoga.

The Song of Naropa reads,

> One cuts off the eight undesirable gates
> And opens up the one desirable one.
> Consciousness becomes the arrow, and energy the bow;
> Thrown by the force of the mantric syllables *HI-KA*,
> Mind fades into the sphere of suchness
> And completes the path of Dharmakaya.
> The name of this technique is the *powa* instruction;
> O Lotsawa, do you have confidence in your mastery of it?

The techniques for closing the eight undesirable passageways whereby consciousness leaves the body at the time of death, and for opening the desirable passageway, are drawn from tantric traditions such as *The Chaturpita Tantra, The Mystic Kiss Tantra,* and so forth. Omniscient Tsongkhapa the Great explains the quintessential instructions of these techniques in his *A Powa Commentary: The Golden Key.*

The basic structure of that process is as follows. One begins by taking refuge in the Buddhas, the Dharma, and the Sangha, and then generating the bodhichitta motivation. This can be done in conjunction with the standard verses or any alternative liturgy. Consecrate the inner offering substances and also the general offerings in accordance with the standard processes used in highest yoga tantra.

Then visualize yourself as Jnana Dakini, a multicolored lotus bearing a moon disc at your heart. Upon this stands the syllable *HUM*. It sends a flood of red beams of light into all directions, which hook and call back myriad Jnana Dakinis inseparable from the guru, surrounded by a host of buddhas, bodhisattvas, dakas, and yoginis. The light rays dissolve into your heart.

Then recite the verse of praise,

> O glorious Vajra Dakini, who turns
> The great wheel of the dakinis,
> And with five wisdoms and three kayas
> Guides living beings: hail to you.

Next make the offerings in the standard manner: *OM SARVA TATHAGATA ARGHAM,* and so forth, until *SHAPTE.* Offer the inner offering by means of the three seed syllables, and then recite the praise:

Homage to the Vajrayogini mandala,
That cuts through the all-pervading cords
That bind living beings in bonds of suffering;
Vajrayogini, who enters into every worldly activity
In order to uplift and liberate living beings.

Now make firm the bodhisattva resolve and meditate on the four immeasurable thoughts of love, compassion, rejoicing in goodness, and equanimity for all living beings. The merit field is delighted and dissolves into you.

Now meditate on the following sadhana. As usual, begin with the emptiness mantra—*OM SHUNYATA JNANA VAJRA SVABHAVA ATMAKO NYA HAM*: All dharmas, being empty of inherent existence, are seen as emptiness.

From within the sphere of emptiness there appears a vajra base, tent, canopy, and mountain of fire. At the center of this is a multicolored lotus bearing a moon disc, and on this stands the mantric syllable *HUM*, white in color. Lights emanate from *HUM*, fulfill the twofold purpose, and absorb back [into *HUM*].

There is complete transformation, and instantly you appear as Jnana Dakini, your body white as the *kunda* flower. You have three faces, each of which has three eyes. The main face is white and is laughing; the right is black and wrathful; and the left is red, with an expression that is both arrogant and lustful.

You have six arms, of which the three hands on the right hold an arrow, a hook, and a vajra, and the three on the left hold a bow, a club made of wood from the wish-fulfilling tree, and the threatening mudra at the heart. You are embellished with all the jewelled ornaments, such as the crown and so forth, and are dressed in exquisite raiments. You are in the warrioress posture, with a white *OM* at your crown, a red *AH* at your throat, and a blue *HUM* at your heart.

Lights emanate from the *HUM* at your heart and summon the Wisdom Beings in the form of Jnana Dakini, and also summon the Initiation Beings. *JAH HUM BAM HOH*: the Wisdom Beings become one with the Samaya Being; the Initiation Beings grant empowerment; Akshobya Buddha becomes your crown ornament.

Then make the offerings with the standard mantra, as follows: *OM JNANA DAKINI SAPARIWARA ARGHAM* [and so forth until] *SHAPTE*. Also make the inner offering, and recite the following verse of praise,

Homage to the Vajrayogini mandala,
That cuts through the all-pervading concepts
That bind living beings in thoughts of suffering;
Vajrayogini, who enters into every worldly activity
In order to uplift and liberate living beings.

Then from within the sphere of visualizing yourself as Jnana Dakini, focus on the three energy channels, together with the four or five chakras. At the point where the central channel terminates at either the navel or secret chakra envision the *AM*-stroke mantric syllable. It is red in color, is extremely hot, and is blazing with the fire of inner heat.

Red lights emanate forth from it and fill your body, from the crown of your head to the soles of your feet, and draw all the vital energies back to it, like smoke from Chinese incense drawn by a draft. It absorbs into the *AM*-stroke syllable at your navel chakra.

Next perform the exclusively tantric form of the vase breathing exercise and establish control over both mind and energy.

At the same time, focus on the syllable *KSHAM*, which is at the mouth of the upper aperture, its head inverted. Below it is a *HUM*, its head inverted. Between the eyebrows is a *HUM*, its head pointed inward. Inside that is a syllable *HAM*, its head inverted. At the root of the tongue is a syllable *SUM*, its head pointed inward. Beside it, in the throat aperture, is the syllable *SMRYUM*, its head inverted. On the pupil of each of the two eyes is a syllable *HUM*; on the doors of the two nostrils and two ears stand syllables of *YAM*, their heads pointing inward. At the navel, and also at the doors of excrement and urine, is a syllable *KSHMRYAM*, its head pointing upward. All of these mantric syllables are white in color and emanate forth extremely thick white light. Meditate that in this way all the bodily apertures are completely blocked off.

Also, on each of your shoulders as armor is a syllable *HMRYUM*, and at your heart is a syllable *YMRYUM*.

After that has been done, concentrate on the inside of the heart chakra, the energy petals of which stretch downward. At that site envision a half moon, which represents the life energy.

Inside of it, in nature your own consciousness, is a syllable *HUM*, its head pointed downward. Above and outside of it are two syllables of *YUM*, a syllable *HI* standing between them. Below and outside the *HUM* are also two syllables of *YUM*, this time with the letter *KA* between them. All seven of these mantric letters are blue in color and stand with their heads pointed downward [i.e., are inverted].

Meditate on this visualization and then engage in the special vase breathing method. As you exhale the breath, imagine that light from the *AM*-stroke syllable at your navel blazes up the central channel and comes to your heart chakra, where it arouses the life energy, carrying the chakra, together with its mantric syllable, upward to your crown. The *HI* and *KA* letters, previously seen as being respectively above and below the inverted *HUM* syllable now reverse positions, with the *HI* below and the *KA* above. As you inhale, the cluster of mantric syllables is drawn back down to the heart chakra, where they appear as previously described.

Repeat this meditation again and again in conjunction with the vase breathing technique, until signs of accomplishment appear. This is how one prepares the consciousness transference passage during one's lifetime by means of practice.

Then when one arrives at the end of one's life and the time of death is at hand, one should distribute one's worldly possessions among worthy recipients and place the mind in a sphere free from attachment and aversion. Make offerings to the dakas, dakinis, and dharmapalas and request blessings that no obstacles may arise.

Visualize that your mandala deity, who is an embodiment of the Three Jewels and is inseparable in nature from your spiritual master, appears in the space in front of you, or above the crown of your head, whichever is easier for you. Offer the seven-limbed devotion, and make the prayer to be guided to the dakini pure lands or to take rebirth as a *vidyadhara*.[10] Perform the special method for applying the vase breathing at the heart chakra, and recite the syllables *HI-KA* twenty-one times. Mind and vital energy, in the form of the cluster of seven syllables visualized at the heart, shoot like a falling star to the heart of the mandala deity inseparable from the guru.

This method of effecting consciousness transference is said to be superior to all others. Its beneficial effects are described in *The Vajradaka Tantra*,

> Killing a brahmin every day,
> Committing any of the five inexpiable acts,
> Stealing and even rape:
> All these karmas are purified through this path.
> One sheds the clothing of guilt for evil deeds done
> And goes far beyond the faults of the world.

With that I will close this treatment of the quintessential points in the practice of the profound instruction known as the Six Yogas of Naropa.

> O hark! Thus is complete my brief treatise, *A Golden Key*,
> To open the door of the vast and profound instruction
> Famed everywhere as the Six Yogas of Glorious Naropa,
> A path that has been traversed by millions of adepts in India
>   and Tibet.
>
> Whatever meritorious energy is born from this composition,
> May the living beings oppressed by the three forms of misery
> Be moved to engage in the ocean of profound trainings;
> May they find freedom and achieve rebirth in the pure realms.

The colophon: This brief treatise for opening a hundred doors leading into the profound path of the Six Yogas of Naropa was written by the Buddhist monk Lobzang Chokyi Gyaltsen, a holder of an ocean of lineages in both the sutra and tantra traditions, at the repeated request of the hermit meditator and monk Ri-tropa Gendun Gyaltsen.

Notes

Translator's Introduction

1. Jey Sherab Gyatso refers to these two texts by slightly different names in Chapter Three: "The textual source of the Six Yogas tradition is the twofold collection known as *The Two Kargyupa Scriptures* (Tib. *bKa' rgyud pa ka dpe gnyis*)." To the best of my knowledge, these have not been openly published and are considered to be extremely secret.

2. The word used for "generation" here does not mean a fixed period of time, but rather refers to thirteen stages in the lineage transmission, i.e., thirteen generations of lineage masters. Each generation dates from the death of one lineage master until the death of his chief disciple. Thus some generations were long and others short, depending upon the lifespan of the individual masters.

3. This of course is just one version of the lineage of transmission, namely, the manner in which it came to Lama Tsongkhapa and the Geluk school. The lineages as preserved in, for example, the Karma Kargyu and Pakmo Drupa Kargyu schools would only be the same in the early generations, until the time of Gampopa. After Gampopa the transmission was carried in many different lineages; each of the four older and eight younger Kargyu schools would have its own lineage from that time onward, passed through the generations of masters of their individual sects.

4. The story of how Marpa Lotsawa received these various tantric transmissions is wonderfully told in his Tibetan biographies. Several of these have been translated into in English. The most extensive is *The Life of Marpa the Translator* (Boulder: Prajna, 1982), translated by the Nalanda Translation Committee.

5. Milarepa says, "First establish the basics, such as Refuge in the Three Jewels, the two aspects of the enlightenment mind—aspirational and engaged—and so forth." His simple words are instructions to cultivate the basic Buddhist foundations.

Refuge in the Three Jewels—the Buddhas, the Dharma and the Sangha—means that one has understood one's basic situation and turned one's life to the spiritual path.

The two bodhiminds—aspirational and engaged—refer to the inner Mahayana perspective. The former is the aspiration to achieve enlightenment as an act of love and compassion for all living beings; the latter refers to cultivating the six perfections—generosity, discipline, gentleness, joyous energy, meditation and wisdom—in order to bring that aspiration to fruition.

6. The oral instruction transmission for achieving liberation in the bardo (Tib. *bar do 'phrang sgrol gyi man ngag*). This name was used for the Six Yogas because by means of these yogas one can achieve enlightenment in any of the three bardos— waking state, sleep state, and after-death state.

One: The Oral Instruction of the Six Yogas

1. The legend of Tilopa's life is wonderfully related in *The Great Kagyu Masters*, by Khenpo Konchok Gyaltsen (Ithaca: Snow Lion Publications, 1990).

2. The lives and lineages of these four masters are told in brief in *The Seven Instruction Lineages*, a translation of Taranatha's *bKa' babs bdun ldan* by David Templeman (Dharamsala, India: LTWA, 1983).

3. Chakrasamvara is the mandala deity that Tilopa used as the basis of his generation stage yoga. This yoga is treated further in Chapter Three, where Jey Sherab Gyatso discusses what mandala deities can be used as the basis of the generation stage practice in the Six Yogas system. A short Chakrasamvara *sadhana* is provided in the introductory section of Tsongkhapa's *A Practice Manual on the Six Yogas*, translated in Chapter Five.

4. Literally "cause and effect." The meaning is that we get specific results from specific endeavors. The result of practicing the Six Yogas of Naropa is the attainment of enlightenment. This extracts "the essence of the human potential."

5. I am translating the Sanskrit term *chandali* as "inner heat." The Tibetan equivalent is *tummo* (*gtum mo*), where the first syllable means "fierce" and refers to the warm bliss that arises from the practice, and the second, a feminine particle, refers to the wisdom that becomes the object of that bliss. *Tum* is male and *mo* female, indicating the necessity of balancing male and female factors—that is, energy and wisdom—in one's training.

6. Krishnacharya is known in Tibetan literature by a number of names, one of which is Charyapa. Another common name for him in Tibetan scriptures is Kanhapada. He is perhaps the most important of the four lineage masters prior to Tilopa from whom the Six Yogas descends, because it is he who synthesized the inner heat teachings of the Hevajra and Heruka Chakrasamvara cycles as transmitted to Tilopa and then Naropa, and as Tsongkhapa states, success in the inner heat yoga is the foundation stone of progress in the remaining five.

His most popular name in Tibetan is Nakpo Chopa (Tib. *Nag po spyod pa*), which means "Black Yogi." Born in the eighth century in Orissa, he embarked upon tantric practice in his youth, first under the guidance of the female mystic

Lakshminkara, and later under the mahasiddha Jalandarapada, the principal disciple of Lawapa. At Jalandarapada's feet he gained great siddhi, such as the powers to fly, walk through solid matter, and so forth. Jalandarapada sent him to study with the female mystic Bhadri, also known as Guhyadakini, and from her he acquired many tantric scriptures, including the *Samputatilika*, and achieved further realization. Jalandarapada then sent him to Oddiyana to receive empowerments from another female mystic, Vajradakini by name, and from her he achieved the ability to travel to the netherworlds, the heavens, and other paranormal realms. He also then achieved the power to transform matter into energy with a single glance. He could tame wild tigers and lions merely by looking at them, and cause mighty soldiers to become frozen into statue-like stillness in his presence.

His guru Jalandarapada, while teaching in eastern India, was captured by a king and buried in a pit for twelve years. When Krishnacharya heard of this he went to the king's palace and sat in meditation. All domesticated animals in the kingdom and all children were unable to drink liquids from the moment he appeared. The king repented and offered food to him and his entourage. Krishnacharya replied, "A poor man like you is unable to fill the bellies of even two of my disciples, let alone all of us." Food for more than a thousand people was prepared, but the two disciples easily consumed it all. The king became his disciple and released his guru Jalandarapada from prison.

When Jalandarapada was offered food he replied, "I have not touched any food or water for the twelve years I sat in meditation in your prison, and have no need for ordinary sustenance now." The king and a thousand of his attendants practiced meditation under the two mahasiddhas and achieved sainthood.

When Krishnacharya eventually passed away he did so by manifesting the rainbow body, that is, dissolving his ordinary aggregates into rainbow light and leaving behind only his hair and nails.

In addition to his role in the Six Yogas transmission, one of the three most important Heruka Chakrasamvara lineages to come to Tibet is rooted in him. The Tibetan canon contains translations of more than seventy-five tantric treatises composed by him in Sanskrit.

7. Tibetans consider both Nagarjuna the second-century Madhyamaka philosopher and Nagarjuna the fifth-century tantric mahasiddha to be one and the same man. According to this account, he taught and wrote about Mahayana Buddhism and Madhyamaka philosophy in his early career and tantric Buddhism in his later years. He achieved the siddhi of immortality, and between the two phases of his teaching life lived in retreat in South India for three hundred years.

Western scholars are skeptical of this legend and believe that there were two Nagarjunas: the first-century Madhyamaka teacher and the fifth-century tantric mahasiddha.

The Nagarjuna referred to in this and the later verse is the tantric mahasiddha.

8. Lawapa (Skt. *Lvavapada*; Tib. *Lva ba pa*) was the guru of Krishnacharya's guru Jalandarapada. Lawapa was a direct disciple of Ghantapada (Tib. *Dril bu pa*). Born as a prince in Oddiyana, he renounced his kingdom for the life of a wandering monk. Eventually he met the mahasiddha Ghantapada, and from him

received the Heruka Chakrasamvara initiation. Thereafter he spent many years meditating in charnel grounds and near cremation pyres.

His name means "the Blanket Master," which he acquired when some proud monks challenged him to debate. He refused to accept their challenge, which angered the local king. The king shouted at him, "Stupid monk, it would be better if you just found somewhere to sleep!" He immediately wrapped himself in his blanket, stretched out on the earth in front of the king's palace, and went to sleep for twelve years without rising. Nobody could walk by him without prostrating, and all who touched his sleeping form were miraculously cured of any illnesses that they had.

When he finally arose from his slumber the king asked him why he had slept so long. "Your Majesty," he replied, "it was your direct command." The king and his court became his disciples.

On another occasion when residing in a charnel ground, 500 black magicians stole his blanket, cut it into small pieces, and ate it as part of a ritual to harm him. He turned their black magic back on them and transformed them into sheep. The king appealed to him to forgive them. He came naked to the court, and had the magicians vomit up his blanket and sew it back together. He then retired to a nearby cave and spent twelve more years in meditation. Here he wrote numerous treatises on tantric practice, many of which are preserved in the Tibetan canon.

9. Sukhasiddhi is one of the great female mystics of late ninth- and early tenth-century Buddhist India. A system of yoga similar to the Naropa tradition is named after her, the Six Yogas of Sukhasiddhi. Several treatises on this yogic legacy exist in Tibetan.

Two: Vajra Verses of the Whispered Tradition

1. The best English-language biography of Naropa is *The Life and Teachings of Naropa* by H. V. Guenther (Oxford: Clarendon Press, 1963).

2. The Tibetan scriptural canon has two wings: the Kangyur, which contains the translations of Buddha's teachings, known as the sutras (exoteric) and tantras (esoteric); and the Tengyur, which contains the Tibetan translations of works by later Indian Buddhist masters, known as *shastras*. Bu-ton Rinchen Drubpa compiled the latter canon. In doing so, he followed strict guidelines of only including texts for which he felt sure that original Sanskrit versions existed. He did not include works created by Tibetan lamas from the direct words of their Indian gurus, for no Sanskrit version of these existed and thus technically they were not "translated shastras."

This is the same Bu-ton Rinchen Drubpa, by the way, who appears in the lineage of transmission of the Six Yogas of Naropa that came to Lama Tsongkhapa as given in the Introduction, and who was the founder of the Zhalu school of Tibetan Buddhism.

The colophon to Naropa's text states, "It is from the mouth of the Indian sage Mahapandita Naropa...." This perhaps suggests that the text was spoken by Naropa directly to Marpa, but was never written out in Sanskrit and therefore did not qualify as a *shastra*. Later editions of the Tengyur, such as that published by Dergey Monastery, from which my English translation was made, added extra titles that Bu-ton had excluded. Some of these probably were texts of which Bu-ton was unaware; others would be texts that he felt were not translations of actual Sanskrit compositions but were written by the Tibetans from notes of their encounters with and teachings received from their Indian gurus.

The First Panchen Lama in his Six Yogas treatise (translated in Chapter Six of this volume) quotes several passages from a text he calls *The Song of Naropa*. This text does not exist in either the Nartang, Dergey, Potala or Peking editions of the Tibetan canon. Presumably Marpa wrote it from Naropa's words directly into Tibetan, without there ever having been a Sanskrit version.

3. The list as given here is from the eighteenth-century Gelukpa lama Ngulchu Dharmabhadra's commentary on Tsongkhapa's *A Book of Three Inspirations*. Ngulchu's text, like that by Jey Sherab Gyatso translated in Chapter Three, is not a commentary written by him, but is a compilation of edited notes from an oral discourse that he gave. It is a brilliant work, taking the very complex text by Tsongkhapa and stripping it down to practical essentials, as well as adding many little-known "asides" about the tradition, such as this list of ten yogas.

4. This passage—"I, Vajradhara, will speak of that auspicious meaning. Offer homage, O Jnana Dakini, and listen well."—probably comes from one of the tantras of the Heruka Chakrasamvara cycle taught by the Buddha in his emanation as Vajradhara. I was unable to locate the exact source. Naropa's meaning is that he is going to paraphrase the meaning of Buddha's tantric teachings in the verses that follow.

5. The Sanskrit term *samaya* was translated into Tibetan as *dam tsig* (*dam tshig*), meaning sacred oath, commitment, or bond. The three sacred commitments of tantric practice are those of the three vehicles: Hinayana, Mahayana, and Vajrayana. The first is to avoid harming any living being; the second is to cultivate the attitude of universal responsibility; and the third is to always cultivate the tantric pride of seeing oneself and all other living beings as sacred mandala deities.

Three: Notes on A Book of Three Inspirations

1. The great guru Drakkar Kachu Rinpochey: Drakkar is the name of an area in Tibet; Kachu is a title meaning "master of the ten instructions"; and Rinpochey means "Precious Teacher." Presumably this is the incarnate lama of the Drakkar region, and the incarnate head of Drakkar Monastery.

2. Jangsem Kunzangpa is another name for Sempa Chenpo Kunzangpa, the editor of Tsongkhapa's *A Practice Manual on the Six Yogas of Naropa*, translated in Chapter Five. "Jangsem" is an abbreviation of Jangchub Sempa, which is the Tibetan equivalent of the Sanskrit word "bodhisattva," meaning "awakening hero." "Sempa Chenpo" means "great hero," which in Sanskrit is Mahasattva. The two are synonymous.

3. Pa Rinto Yontsang and Gyalsey Rinpochey: I don't know who the first lama is; the latter is a famous incarnate lama of Drepung Loseling Monastery, and also

the incarnate head of Tawang Monastery, located at the birthplace of the Sixth Dalai Lama in modern-day Arunachal Pradesh, India. Until 1914 this part of India belonged to Tibet; it was lost to British India at the time of the 1913-14 Shimla Agreement. The 1962 war between India and China was fought over this disputed territory.

The present Gyalsey Rinpochey incarnation lives and teaches in Tawang Monastery.

4. *A Thousand Blazing Sunbeams* (Tib. *'Od zer stong 'bar*): A text on the Six Yogas popular as a teaching tool with the earlier Kargyupa lamas. I am unsure of the authorship, as I was unable to locate a copy.

5. This is the literal translation. The meaning is (1) meditations that cause the mind to develop spiritual inclinations; (2) meditations that cause spiritual inclinations to transform into spiritual experience; (3) meditations that cause spiritual experience to pacify the emotional and mental/spiritual distortions; and (4) meditations that cause the distorted mind to arise as wisdom.

In many of the Kargyu schools today these four stages of training, which involve dozens of meditative and contemplative techniques, are used to accomplish the inner foundations on which tantric practice can be successfully engaged.

6. In the Kadam and Geluk, and to some extent also in the Kargyu and Sakya schools, the Lamrim tradition brought to Tibet by Atisha Dipamkara Shrijnana in 1042 is used as the practice guide to the General Mahayana trainings in order to prepare the mind for tantra.

The three levels of the Lamrim training are simply called initial, intermediate and advanced. The initial level is comprised of meditations for turning the mind from negative action and materialistic grasping, and instead replacing these negative states with the aspiration to goodness and higher rebirth. The intermediate level training is comprised of meditations for turning the mind from grasping at higher sensual and meditative pleasures and engendering the aspiration to nirvana. The advanced level of training is comprised of meditations for turning the mind from self-grasping and engendering the bodhisattva mind of universal love.

Tsongkhapa wrote three Lamrim treatises on these meditations, the longest of which is over 500 folios, or 1,000 pages in length.

7. Tsongkhapa presents meditational outlines for both of these methods in his *A Practice Manual on the Six Yogas*.

8. Again, these can be seen in Tsongkhapa's *A Practice Manual on the Six Yogas*.

9. The three kayas are discussed in Chapter Four.

10. At a public teaching the present Dalai Lama gave on *A Book of Three Inspirations* in Dharamsala, 1991, he commented that the term *kyawa* (Tib. *rkya ba*) used here can also refer to the oars; just as one needs to keep the two oars moving with equal strength, one needs to put equal emphasis on the conventional and ultimate levels of reality.

11. Tsongkhapa explains the correct manner of envisioning the chakras in *A Practice Manual on the Six Yogas*.

12. A translation of a treatise on the Six Yogas of Niguma is included in my study on the life and teachings of the Second Dalai Lama, *Selected Works of the Dalai Lama II* (Snow Lion, 1984).

13. The second of these two texts, that by Panchen Chogyen, is translated in Chapter Six of this volume.

14. This is one of the high incarnate lamas of Ganden Jangtsey Monastery. His most recent incarnation passed away in Nepal in 1995.

15. Kyabgon Dorjey Chang is a familiar honorific for a high lama, and simply means "All-Pervading Buddha Vajradhara." At any one time there are a dozen Gelukpa lamas known by this name. The disciples attending Jey Sherab Gyatso's discourse would have known the person to whom it referred, as he would have been one of Sherab Gyatso's main gurus.

16. I presume this refers to the First Panchen Lama, but it could also mean the Panchen who was a contemporary of Jey Sherab Gyatso.

Four: Handprints of the Profound Path of the Six Yogas of Naropa

1. There are two ways of listing the successive incarnations of the Panchen lamas, due to the three important pre-Panchen incarnations. When these three are added in, the First Panchen Lama becomes the Fourth in the line, and Gyalwa Wensapa then becomes the Third.

The Lhasa government, however, who keeps the "official list," counts Panchen Chokyi Gyaltsen (1568-1662) as the First Panchen Lama, and the Panchen Lama who died in Tibet in 1989 as the seventh incarnation. For most Tibetans, therefore, Gyalwa Wensapa is not considered an official Panchen Lama.

This situation with two different lists was not the case in the early days, and seems to have arisen in the early 1800s, when the Ninth to Twelfth Dalai Lamas died young, and the Panchen became a very important figure in Tibetan affairs. His numbering was increased by three in order to add prestige to the office.

The Chinese follow the tradition of giving the larger number to the incarnations, on the basis that more is better. The Tibetans list the Panchen who died in 1989 as the seventh incarnation (Tib. *sku 'phreng bdun pa*); the Chinese list him as the tenth (Tib. *sku 'phreng bcu pa*). Similarly, by Lhasa reckoning the present young incarnation is counted as the eighth; by Chinese reckoning he is the eleventh.

As Tibet-watchers will be aware, the Tibetan child recognized as the Eighth Panchen Lama by the Dalai Lama in May of 1995 was immediately arrested and imprisoned by the Chinese government, who in turn recognized and enthroned their own candidate several months later, in December of 1995. In that Chinese Communists do not acknowledge the doctrine of reincarnation, their role in overseeing the search for and enthronement of an official reincarnate lama has not gone down well with the Tibetans. Even as I write, however, Beijing's government is giving all monks in Tibet the option of either signing a document acknowledging Beijing's candidate and repudiating the Dalai Lama's candidate, or else facing expulsion from their monasteries and also possible imprisonment and torture.

Thus today there are two Panchen Lamas: the child installed by the Chinese Communists; and the child recognized a year earlier by the Dalai Lama, who, together with his parents and forty-eight monks from Tashi Lhunpo who participated in the search, languish in prison or under house arrest. None of these religious prisoners has been seen or heard from since their arrest. The child has been adopted by Amnesty International as the world's youngest political prisoner.

2. See *Tsongkhapa's Six Yogas of Naropa* (Snow Lion, 1996), pp. 188-190.

3. Vajradhara is the name given to Buddha in his primordial tantric emanation. "The myriads of mandala deities" refers to the manner in which Buddha in his form as Vajradhara manifested as various tantric deities and taught the different tantric systems.

4. These twelve are as follows: an illusory appearance (Tib. *sgyu ma*), objects in a dream (Tib. *rmi lam*), an hallucination (Tib. *mig sgyu*), a reflection in a mirror (Tib. *gzugs brnang*), lightning in the sky (Tib. *glog*), an echo in a cave (Tib. *brag cha*), a rainbow (Tib. *'ja' tshon*), the moon in a lake (Tib. *chu zla*), a city of ghosts (Tib. *dri za'i grong khyer*), cloud-forms that deceive the eye (Tib. *mig yor sprin*), and magically emanated forms (Tib. *sprul pa*).

5. Emotional obscurations: Skt. *klesha avarana*; Tib. *nyon sgrib.*

6. Perceptual obscurations: Skt. *nyer avarana*; Tib. *shes sgrib.*

7. Basowa Tenpai Gyaltsen was Gyalwa Wensapa's chief disciple, and is also reputed to have achieved enlightenment in one lifetime.

Five: A Practice Manual on the Six Yogas of Naropa

1. Even though Tsongkhapa's text is very different from that by Gyalwa Wensapa translated in the previous chapter, this aspect of his outline resembles Wensapa's analysis of how the Six Yogas involve two main techniques—those for bringing the energies into the central channel; and those to be applied once the energies have been brought into the central channel. Wensapa, however, spoke of these two subjects in terms of the principles of the three blendings; Tsongkhapa will describe the actual meditations whereby these two stages are accomplished.

2. The idea of the navel channel-petals reaching up and those of the heart down, and also those of the throat chakra reaching up and those of the crown reaching down, is that there are two pairs of chakras—the crown/throat set and the heart/navel set—with each pair being comprised of one male and one female chakra that arouse and stimulate one another. The male is on top in both sets; female heat rises and male fluids flow down.

3. That is, it is a vertical line, but it is thicker at the base and becomes increasingly thinner as it rises, somewhat like a thorn or toothpick standing on its thick end.

4. The male and female "drops" that flow through the body are termed *bodhichitta* in Sanskrit, meaning "enlightenment substances." *Bodhi* means enlightenment, and *chitta* means mind. Following the lead of the late great Geshey Wangyal, I translate the term bodhichitta as "bodhimind" when it appears in a Sutrayana context, and as "bodhimind substances" when it appears in a tantric context.

5. Sometimes the mantric syllable at the navel is called *AH* and sometimes *AM*, due to the presence of the crescent above it. The visualization is identical for both, and thus both transcriptions of the mantra are correct. Either way it is just a vertical stroke with the three-piece crescent above it.

6. *Kyurura* is a type of transparent fruit that glistens and shines when held in the light.

7. These "elemental dissolutions" together with the four "sky-like signs" are discussed in the preamble to Chapter Four.

8. These "three blendings" were the subject of Gyalwa Wensapa's text, translated in Chapter Four.

9. The four types of birth in the Buddhist world view are (1) birth from a womb, (2) birth from an egg, (3) birth from a fusion of heat and moisture, and (4) miraculous birth. All living beings take birth in one of these four ways.

10. That is, one's five skandhas: one's sense of form, feelings, distinguishing awareness, mental/metaphysical archetypes, and primary consciousnesses. A "person" is the sense of "I" that arises from these five. Our entire experience of the world and of life is known by means of them.

11. That is, the level of the illusory body accomplishment that is concomitant with the attainment of "the path of direct vision," the third of the five stages leading to enlightenment. On this level the yogi or yogini has direct insight into emptiness, or ultimate reality, during meditation sessions, and has become an arya, or saint. When exiting from meditation and engaging in activities on the conventional level, the practitioner loses the direct vision of emptiness; therefore the path above this is known as "the path of integration," because from this point on the process of growth involves integrating the two levels of reality into a unified vision.

12. This is the same posture as that in which the Buddha passed away, and therefore is the subject of considerable artistic activity. Most Buddhist temples around the world have a painting or statue of the Buddha lying in this posture.

13. Tsongkhapa does describe the technique in depth in *A Book of Three Inspirations*, translated in *Tsongkhapa's Six Yogas of Naropa* (Snow Lion, 1996). Jey Sherab Gyatso also discusses it briefly in the text translated in Chapter Three of the present volume.

Six: The Golden Key

1. According to Tibetan rumor, the Seventh Panchen Lama died from poison administered by the Chinese Communists a few days after a public talk that he gave, in which he condemned the Chinese presence in Tibet and said, "There is nothing that the Communists could ever do now to compensate for the tremendous destruction and suffering that their occupation has incurred." Four days later he died mysteriously during the night.

2. These were discussed by Jey Sherab Gyatso in the text that appears here as Chapter Three.

3. Jey Sherab Gyatso discussed the general principles of the generation stage yogas in Chapter Three. Tsongkhapa's text in Chapter Five provides a brief Heruka Chakrasamvara *sadhana* that can be used as the basis of the generation stage meditations.

4. The introductory sections of Tsongkhapa's text in Chapter Five provide brief meditation instructions for both the Vajrasattva and guru yoga practices, under the heading "The Special Tantric Preliminaries."

Jey Sherab Gyatso briefly discusses the topics of refuge and the bodhisattva perspective. Readers who want more explanation of the traditional meditations associated with these two subjects can read one of my earlier books with Snow Lion Publications, *Training the Mind in the Great Way* (1993), which contains the First Dalai Lama's treatise on the Tibetan contemplative system known as "Seven Points for Training the Mind in the Mahayana Tradition" (Tib. *Theg chen blo sbyong don bdun ma*).

5. As I mentioned in the Introduction, there are several Tibetan texts by this name (Tib. *Na ro'i mgur*) attributed to Naropa. The original Tengyur compiled by Buton does not include any of them, and the Tengyur published several centuries later by Dergey Monastery includes only the one that I have translated in Chapter Two of the present volume.

This passage by the First Panchen Lama may be a reference to that work. However, later in this text the First Panchen Lama quotes another "Song of Naropa" which is a different work altogether, and is not found in any of the Tibetan canonical collections. This passage may also be a reference to that second text.

With the dispersion of Tibetan literature caused by the Chinese destruction of Tibet's great libraries it is difficult to know what from among this little-known body of writings has been lost, and also very difficult to know what still survives and where it is to be found. Very few of the existing reservoirs of Tibetan literature have catalogues of their holdings.

6. The First Panchen Lama has lifted this and the previous verse by Marpa Lotsawa from Tsongkhapa's *A Book of Three Inspirations*. Tsongkhapa in turn probably lifted them from the official biography of Marpa. An English translation of this exists, prepared by the Nalanda Translation Committee (*The Life of Marpa the Translator* [Boulder: Prajna Press, 1982]).

7. The four descending blisses occur when the inner heat yoga causes the drop to descend from the crown to the jewel chakra; as it passes through each of the four chakras it causes an increasingly intense sensation of orgasmic bliss. This drop is then brought back up from the jewel to the crown chakra, giving rise to the four ascending blisses. Tsongkhapa describes the meditations that accomplish this process in *A Practice Manual on the Six Yogas*.

8. "Clarifying the breath and bodily energies" refers to the nine-point breathing exercise and six physical exercises, described in Tsongkhapa's *A Practice Manual on the Six Yogas*.

9. Seeing oneself as Nirmanakaya means seeing oneself as the mandala deity. The Jnanasattva at one's heart means establishing the radiant mantric syllable *HUM* in the heart chakra.

10. The term *vidyadhara* translates literally as "knowledge holder." This refers to taking a controlled rebirth as a tantric master in order to perform vast and extensive activities for the benefit of the world.

Glossary:

Tibetan Personal and Place Names

Anglicization	*Tibetan spelling*
Basowa Tenpai Gyaltsen	Ba so ba bsTan pa'i rgyal mtshan
Bonpo	Bon po
Bu-ton Rinchen Drup	Bu ston Rin chen sgrub
Chojey Sonam Gyaltsen	Chos rje bSod nams rgyal mtshan
Chokyi Dorjey	Chos kyi rdo rje
Dakpo	Dvags po
Darma Dodey	Dar ma mdo sde
Drakkar Kachu Rinpochey	Brag dkar bKa' bcu Rin po che
Drikung	'Bri gung
Drikung Jigten Sumgon	'Bri gung 'Jig rten gsum dgon
Drukpa Kargyupa	'Brug pa bka' brgyud pa
Gampopa	sGam po pa
Galuk	dGa' lugs
Ganden	dGa' ldan
Ganden Shartsey	dGa' ldan shar rtse
Geluk	dGe lugs
Goe Lotsawa	'Gos Lo ts› ba
Gyalpo	rGyal po
Gyalsey Rinpochey	rGyal sras Rin po che
Gyaltsab Jey	rGyal tshab rje
Gyalwa	rGyal ba
Gyalwa Gendun Gyatso	rGyal ba dGe 'dun rgya mtsho
Gyalwa Nyipa	rGyal ba gnyis pa
Gyalwa Wensapa	rGyal ba dBen sa pa
Halha Zhab-drung	Ha hla Zhabs 'drung
Jampa Palwa	Byams pa dpal ba

Jangsem Kunzangpa	Byang sems kun bzang pa
Jetsun	rJe btsun
Jetsun Basowa	rJe btsun Ba so ba
Jetsun Lobzang Yeshey	rJe btsun Blo bzang ye shes
Jetsun Milarepa	rJe btsun Mi la ras pa
Jey Sherab Gyatso	rJe Shes rab rgya mtsho
Jigten Sumgon	'Jig rten gsum dgon
Kadam	bKa' gdams
Kajou Zhing	mKha' spyod zhing
Kargyu	bKa' brgyud
Kargyupa	bKa' brgyud pa
Karmapa	bKar ma pa
Kham	Khams
Khedrup Gelek Palzangpo	mKhas grub dGe legs dpal bzang po
Khedrup Jampa Pel	mKhas grub Byams pa dpal
Khedrup Norzang Gyatso	mKhas grub Nor bzang rgya mtsho
Kyabgon Dorjey Chang	sKyab mgon rdo rje 'chang
Langdol Lama	Klong rdol bla ma
Lawapa	La bva pa
Lhasa	Hla sa
Lobzang Chogyen	Blo bzang chos rgyan
Lobzang Drakpa	Blo bzang grags pa
Lodrak	Hlo brag
Lodrak Drowolung	Hlo brag gro bo lung
Lotsawa	Lo ts› ba
Lubum Ritropa	Glu 'bum ri khrod pa
Lobzang Dondrub	Blo bzang don grub
Luipa	Lu'i pa
Maitripa	Mee tri pa
Marpa Lodrakpa	Mar pa Hlo brag pa
Chokyi Lotru	Chos kyi blo gros
Maryul Loden	Mar yul blo ldan
Menkangpa	sMan khang pa
Milarepa	Mi la ras pa
Miwang Drakpa Gyaltsen	Mi dbang Grags pa rgyal mtshan
Monlam Chenmo	sMon lam chen mo
Ngawang Palden	Ngag dbang dpal ldan
Ngulchu Dharmabhadra	dNgul chu Dhar ma bha dra
Nyingma	rNying ma
Olkha	dBol kha
Pa Rinto Yontsang	Pa rin tho yon tshang
Pakmo Drupa	Phag mo gru pa
Paljor Rabten	dPal 'byor rab brtan
Palkor Chodey	dPal 'khor chos sde
Panchen Chogyen	Pan chen Chos rgyan
Panchen Tamchey Khyenpa	Pan chen Thams cad mkhyen pa

Rinpochey	Rin po che
Sakya	Sa skya
Samyey Chimpu	bSam yas mchim phu
Sangyey Yeshey	Sang rgyas ye shes
Sempa Chenpo Kunzangpa	Sems dpa' chen po kun bzang pa
Sonam Gyaltsen	bSod nams rgyal mtshan
Sonam Sengey	bSod nams seng ge
Sonam Wangpo	bSod nams dbang po
Tang Sakpa	Thang sag pa
Tashi Lhunpo	bKra' shis hlun po
Tilbupa	Dril bu pa
Tsang	gTsan
Tsongkhapa	Tsong kha pa Blo bzang grags pa
Vajradhara Lobzang Dondrup	rDo rje 'chang Blo bzang don grub
Wensapa Lobzang Dondrup	dBen sa pa Blo bzang don grub
Wonton Kyergangwa	dBon ston sKyer sgang ba
Yang Gonpa	Yang dgon pa
Zhalu	Zha lu

Texts Quoted by the Authors

INDIAN TEXTS

The Advaya Vijaya Tantra
   Tib. Canon: dPal de bzhin gshegs pa thams cad kyi gsang ba rnal 'byor chen
      po rnam par rgyal ba zhes bya ba mnyam pa nyid gnyis su med pa'i rgyud
      kyi rgyal po rdo rje dpal mchog chen po brtag pa dang po
   Skt. Śrī-sarvatathāgata-guhyatantra-yoga-mahā-rajā-advayasamatā-vijaya-
      nāma-vajra-śrī-paramamahākalpa-ādi
   Tripitaka # 88
   Author: Buddha

Arising of Samvara Tantra
   Tib. Canon: dPal bde mchog 'byung ba zhes bya ba'i rgyud kyi rgyal po chen po
   Skt. Śrī-mahāsaṃvarodaya-tantrarāja-nāma
   Tripitaka # 20
   Author: Buddha

The Chakrasamvara Root Tantra
   Tib. Canon: rGyud kyi rgyal po dpal bde mchog nyung ngu zhes bya ba
   Skt. Tantrarāja-śrī-laghusaṃvara-nāma
   Tripitaka # 16
   Author: Buddha

The Chaturpita Tantra
   Tib. Canon: dPal gdan bzhi pa'i rnam par bshad pa'i rgyud kyi rgyal po zhes
      bya ba
   Skt. Śrī-caturpīṭha-vikhyāta-tantrarāja-nāma
   Tripitaka # 69
   Author: Buddha

The Clear Lamp
Tib. Canon: sGron ma gsal bar byed pa zhes bya ba'i rgya che bshad pa
Skt. Pradipoddyotana-nama-tika
Tripitaka # 2650
Author: Chandrakirti

A Compendium of Tantric Experiences
Tib. Canon: sPyod pa bsdus pa'i sgron ma
Skt. Caryā-melāpaka-pradīpa
Tripitaka # 2668
Author: Āryadeva

Elucidation of the Summary of the Five Stages
Tib. Canon: Rim pa lnga'i don gsal bar byed pa zhes bya ba
Skt. Pañcakramārtha-bhāskaraṇa-nāma
Tripitaka # 2702
Author: Nāgabodhi

Fifty Verses on the Guru
Tib. Canon: Bla ma lnga bcu pa zhes bya ba
Skt. Guru-pañcāśikā
Tripitaka # 4544
Author: Aśvaghoṣa

The Five Stages
Tib. Canon: Rim pa lnga pa zhes bya ba
Skt. Pañca-krama
Tripitaka # 2667
Author: Nāgārjuna

The Four Seats Tantra
Tib. Canon: dPal gdan bzhi pa'i rnam par bshad pa'i rgyud kyi rgyal po zhes
bya ba
Skt. Śrī-caturpīṭha-vikhyāta-tantrarāja-nāma
Tripitaka # 69
Author: Buddha

The Guhyasamaja Tantra
Tib. Canon: De bzhin gshegs pa thams cad kyi sku gsung thugs kyi gsang
chen gsang ba 'dus pa zhes bya ba brtag pa'i rgyal po chen po
Skt. Sarvatathāgata-kāya-vāk-citta-rahasyo guhyasamāja-nāma-mahā-
kalparāja
Tripitaka # 81
Author: Buddha

Heruka Chakrasamvara Tantra
See *The Chakrasamvara Root Tantra*

Hevajra Tantra
See *Hevajra Tantra in Two Sections*

The Hevajra Tantra in Two Sections
   Tib. Canon: Kye'i rdo rje zhes bya ba rgyud kyi rgyal po
   Skt. Hevajra-tantrarāja-nāma
   Tripitaka # 10
   Author: Buddha

The Mark of Mahamudra
   Tib. Canon: dPal phyag rgya chen po'i thig le zhes bya ba rnal 'byor ma chen
      mo'i rgyud kyi rgyal po mnga' bdag
   Skt. Śrī-mahāmudrātilikaṃ-nāma-yoginī-tantrarāja-adhipati
   Tripitaka # 12
   Author: Buddha

The Mystic Kiss Tantra
   Tib. Canon: rNal 'byor ma bzhi'i kha sbyor gyi rgyud ces bya ba
   Skt. Catur-yoginī-saṃpuṭa-tantra-nāma
   Tripitaka # 24
   Author: Buddha

Prajnaparamita Sutra in 100,000 Verses
   Tib. Canon: Shes rab kyi pha rol tu phyin pa 'bum ba'i mdo
   Skt. Prajñāpāramitāśatasāhasrikāsūtra
   Tripitika # 730
   Author: Buddha

The Samputa Tantra
   Tib. Canon: Yang dag par sbyor ba zhes bya ba'i rgyud chen po
   Skt. Saṃpuṭi-nāma-mahātantra
   Tripitaka # 26
   Author: Buddha

Sixty Stanzas on Emptiness
   Tib. Canon: Rigs pa drug bcu pa'i tshig le'ur byas ba zhes bya ba
   Skt. Yuktiṣaṣtikā-kārikā-nāma
   Tripitaka # 5225
   Author: Nāgārjuna

Ten Reflections on Simple Suchness
   Tib. Canon: De kho na nyid bcu pa zhes bya ba
   Skt. Tattvadaśaka-nāma
   Tripitaka # 3080
   Author: Advayavajra [Maitripa]

Ten Reflections on Simple Suchness: A Commentary
   Tib. Canon: De kho na nyid bcu pa rgya cher 'grel pa
   Skt. Tattva-daśaka-ṭīkā
   Tripitaka # 3099
   Author: Sahajavajra

Treasury of Abhidharma
Tib. Canon: Chos mngon pa'i mdzod kyi tshig le'ur byas pa
Skt. Abhidharma-koṣa-kārikā
Tripitaka # 5590
Author: Vasubandhu

The Vajradaka Tantra
Tib. Canon: dPal rdo rje mkha' 'gro gsang ba'i rgyud kyi rgyal po
Skt. Śrī-vajraḍākaguhya-tantrarāja
Tripitaka # 44
Author: Buddha

The Vajramala Tantra
Tib. rNal 'byor chen po'i rgyud dpal rdo rje phreng ba mngon par brjod pa
    rgyud thams cad kyi snying po gsang ba rnam par phye ba zhes bya ba
Skt. Śrī-vajramāla-abhidāna-mahāyogatantra sarvatantrahṛdaya-rahasya-
    vibhaṅga-iti
Tripitaka # 82
Author: Buddha

Vajra Song of the Six Dharmas
Tib. Canon: Chos drug gi man ngag ces bya ba
Skt. Ṣaddharmopadeśa-nāma
Tripitaka # 4630
Author: Nāropa

TIBETAN TEXTS

*A Book of Three Inspirations: A Treatise on the Stages of Training in the Profound
    Path of Naropa's Six Yogas*
Tib. Zab lam na ro'i chos drug gi sgo nas 'khrid pa'i rim pa yid ches gsum ldan
Author: Tsongkhapa

A Clear Lamp on the Five Stages
Tib. Rim lnga gsal sgron
Author: Tsongkhapa

A Clear Lamp on the Precepts
Tib. Dam tshig gsal sgron
Author: Khedrup Norzang Gyatso

A Commentary on Consciousness Transference Yoga
Tib. 'Pho ti ka
Author: Tsongkhapa

The Complete Seat
Tib. gDan rdzogs
Author: Tsongkhapa

Early Compendium Root Text
 Tib. Ka dpe rtsa ba'i sdom snga ma
 Author: various, as it is a compendium

Eight Instructions
 Tib. Tshig rkang brgyad ma
 Author: Marpa Lotsawa

Later Compendium Root Text
 Tib. Ka dpe rtsa ba'i sdom phyi ma
 Author: various, as it is a compendium

A Powa Commentary: The Golden Key
 See *A Commentary on Consciousness Transference Yoga*

A Practice Manual On the Six Yogas of Naropa: Taking the Practice in Hand
 Tib. Zab lam na ro'i chos drug gi dmigs skor lag tu len tshul
 Author: Tsongkhapa

Two Kargyupa Scriptures
 Tib. bKa' rgyud pa ka dpe gnyis
 Author: various, as they are compendiums